Cast A Cold Eye

Memories of a poet's son and politician

Cast A Cold Eye

Memories of a poet's son and politician

by

Michael B. Yeats

Editor
Margaret Burns

Design & Layout
Paula Byrne

Cover Design

ISBN
0 86121 968 6

Produced in Ireland by
Blackwater Press
c/o Folens Publishers
8 Broomhill Business Park,
Tallaght, Dublin 24.

Contents

Preface

That this book exists is due to the urgings of my family and various friends, who over the years would listen to my memories and say, 'You really should be writing all this down'. Then one year the family got together and bought me a word processor. Nothing was said about the reason for this gift, but the implications were obvious. In the end it seemed easier to write the book than to keep on producing reasons for not doing so.

Before I began writing, I laid down some ground rules for myself. This would not be an autobiography. I would of course be expected to write about my upbringing in a most unusual family, but I decided that once that was done I would turn away from purely personal matters. I would thenceforth write about what has most interested me, the new nation that was developing all around me. I was born just a few months before the Anglo-Irish Treaty of 1921, so my lifetime has coincided with that of the Irish State.

For some forty years I was involved in public life – in Ireland, and later on in the European Community. I watched with interest as history was being made around me, and I 'cast a cold eye' on some of those who made it. What I have written in this book is one man's view of our modern political history.

Early Memories

'What is it like to be the son of a great poet?' I have often been asked. What can I say? I might just as well ask in return, 'what is it like to have a father who is a civil servant, or a teacher, or a farmer?' And I might ask further, 'what is it like to have a father who is young and energetic, plays with the children, goes on picnics with them, takes an active part in family discipline?' None of this did I ever experience as a child. Nor did it even occur to me that that was what a 'normal' family was like. My father, William Butler Yeats, married very late in life, and was 56 years old when I was born in 1921. By the time I was 10 years old and began to take an intelligent interest in events around me, he was 66 and in increasingly poor health.

My mother, who was English, was 27 years younger than he was, and in effect was in complete control of the household. From the first, she had accepted that her mission in life was to ensure that nothing would interfere with the production of great poetry for the world. 'Now, children, don't make a noise; your father is working', was the refrain heard from our earliest years by my elder sister, Anne, and myself. Not that in any way we were neglected. We had a nurse, Florence Reade, who looked after us, and my mother ensured our continued well-being: but nonetheless we were kept apart from the ordinary, day-to-day life of the family. All the great literary and artistic figures of the day visited our house, as well as numerous politicians, but we never met these, though we occasionally watched them come and go, from a distance.

My very early years were spent mainly in a large Georgian house in Merrion Square in Dublin, the first of a number of houses in which we lived during my childhood. I remember little of this period, save for some early flashes of memory. I must have been very young indeed when I looked over the edge of my pram and admired the nice new white tyres that had been fitted to the wheels. There was a day when word came out that Government Buildings were on fire. We were brought round the corner to view the scene, and I remember my disappointment when there was nothing to be seen – no fire, not even smoke – just a few fire engines standing around.

A greater influence was Ballylee Castle, near Gort, in Co. Galway, where we spent part of each year. In every year since 1896 my father had made extended visits to Lady Augusta Gregory, his great friend, mentor and collaborator in the foundation of the Abbey Theatre, at her house at Coole Park, just a few miles from Ballylee. She was of the Persse family, whose Roxborough estates were nearby, and who were notoriously bad landlords, but she herself adopted nationalist views, and learned the Irish language.

Lady Gregory brought my father from house to house collecting folklore, and in particular he learned about the blind poet Anthony Raftery, and the song he wrote, 'Máire Ní Eidhin', about the beautiful Mary Hynes, who lived, and died young, at Ballylee. When my father first went to Ballylee he was told about her by people who still remembered her, and he was shown the ruins of her house.

Many years later he still remembered these things when he decided to buy Ballylee Castle. He negotiated at length with the Congested Districts Board, who in the end sold him the Castle and two attached cottages for the munificent sum of £35. It seems that after the Gregory estate had been divided no one else wanted an old Norman tower with just a half acre of land surrounding it. Besides the connection with Mary Hynes, my father was attracted to the tower because it was a wonderfully romantic place, a perfect home for a poet, set in the beautiful Kiltartan countryside, quiet, surrounded by trees, with a river flowing underneath the tower window. A further attraction was that it was ideally situated, just a few miles from Coole Park. He spent part of the proceeds of an American lecture tour on repairing the buildings, and he and my mother spent their first summer there in 1919, with Anne, then a baby just a few months old.

Ballylee was a more attractive place for a young child than the house in Dublin had ever been. The river flowing past the tower, the bridge, the little shed opposite where we could watch the dead hens being plucked, were all of interest. There was the little cottage up the road where an eccentric old lady lived. She used to brush her teeth in the middle of the road outside, and when asked why, explained that she had to because of the ogre under her bed. We did not see much of the interior of the tower, possibly because it was where my father was, and so children were not encouraged, in case they might interfere with the writing of poetry.

In fact we saw little of the poet in those early years. He was pleased to have a family, but he had really no idea of how to deal with very small children. There is a well-known photograph, taken at Ballylee, of my father sitting in a field, flanked by my sister and myself. This has been accepted by generations of scholars as a perhaps rare example of the poet as a family man, but in fact the reality is somewhat different. My mother had arranged for a professional to come out from Gort to take some photographs of the tower, and she told my father that she wanted one taken with the children. He had been reading a book, but, as can be seen in the photograph, he put it down carefully on the ground, open with the spine upwards so that he would not lose his place. Once the photograph had been taken and the children removed, he resumed his interrupted reading.

Ballylee may have been a wonderful place for children, and also of course for poets; but it was less so for housewives. The nearest shop was in Gort, 4 miles away, so that even the simplest item, such as a loaf of bread, had to be got from there. I am sure my mother had most things delivered, but anything extra, or that had been forgotten, meant an 8-mile bicycle trip. In those days Ballylee was a remote spot: there were few cars, and the only real connections with the outside world were the train to Athenry and Dublin from Gort, and the telegraph. There was of course no telephone at Ballylee, nor running water, nor electricity.

Another problem at Ballylee was flooding. The river that runs past the tower disappears about a half mile downstream into a hole in the ground; and of course the hole remains the same size in times of flood, so that the excess water has nowhere to go but up. On such occasions the ground floor of the tower and the two cottages attached to it would be covered by up to

3 feet of muddy water. Anne and I would be packed off to Lady Gregory's nearby house at Coole Park, the poet would retreat to an upper floor in the Tower, and my mother would deal with the situation as best she could until the waters receded. Then she would clean things up, sweep the mud and wriggling worms out through the door; then the great man would descend and life would resume.

These floods may have been caused by the drainage of the Gregory estate through which the river ran. Before drainage, the excess water was probably absorbed by the marshland. Afterwards it ran straight through – hence the flooding. The people of the area were well used to all this, and the miller just down the road kept a boat which he used to escape from his upper window, when necessary.

The presence of all this water may have been what persuaded my father that we ought to acquire a duck-house. But when he made this suggestion to my mother she resisted the idea – knowing perfectly well that it would not be the poet who would look after the ducks. He kept on coming back to this question, but my mother stayed firm, and for a few months there was no further mention of ducks. Then one day he asked 'George, what colour did we say we'd paint the duck-house? – Oh, I'm sorry, I forgot we're not going to have any ducks.' At that my mother gave in, and in due course we had a duck-house with two ducks that each night had to be manoeuvred into it by my mother, with some assistance from my sister, Anne.

There were other problems in the early years of our visits to Ballylee. When we were small, Anne and I slept in one of the thatched cottages in cradles, on which the rats would run at night, until their various entrances and exits had been found and plugged. Another difficulty in early days was created by the thatched roof of the cottages. Birds and other forms of animal life would settle in the thatch, and all sorts of objectionable things would drop down. As a result my mother had a ceiling put in.

The big room that filled the whole ground floor of the tower had a wooden ceiling that my mother had painted in a number of different colours, red, white, green, blue, yellow, etc. There was a reason for this. At the time she was painting the ceiling, around the year 1920, there was gunfire in the neighbourhood. One afternoon she ran out of paint and, rather than take the risk of cycling into Gort to buy some more, she used up the remains of some old paint pots that were lying around.

One day in 1923, during the Civil War period, three men arrived and explained that they needed to blow up the bridge which lay just 10 feet or so from the tower. According to my parents, the whole thing was arranged on a most friendly basis, and when the charges had been laid one man remained behind, handing out balls of cotton wool to protect the ears of the family. Being only a baby at the time, I have no memory of this event, but I do remember the temporary repairs carried out by the local people about a year later, with large tree trunks being used to fill in the gap that had been made by the explosion. Before the repair there had been just sufficient left of the bridge for a horse and cart to cross with some difficulty. My sister Anne, who was a couple of years older and had thus reached a more bloodthirsty age, remembers sitting by the bridge before the repair, waiting patiently in the hope that a cart would fall into the stream.

Shortly after the blowing up of the bridge at Ballylee – when I was still under two years old – I became ill, and had to be taken to Dublin urgently for an operation. But all the roads between the tower and the main roads were blocked, and so access to Gort railway station seemed impossible. Fortunately the local taxi was also shut in, and its driver agreed to try to make the journey. So we set off, driving across the fields in the taxi, with my mother carrying me, and with us the local Parish Priest, who also wanted to go to Dublin. Each time we reached one of the Galway dry stone walls, my mother and the driver got out and dismantled the wall; he drove through, and they then built up the wall again. My mother never forgave the Parish Priest, who sat in the car throughout, doing nothing to help. In due course they all reached Gort, and thence to Dublin, which may be why I survived to write this book.

We had few visitors at Ballylee, unlike our Dublin house. There was, however, at least one visitor who came to dinner, the local Church of Ireland curate. Lady Gregory heard of this event, and took my mother aside. Always anxious to ensure that the great poet's new young English wife understood properly the customs of the country in which she now lived, she set out to explain. 'One invites the curate to afternoon tea', she said, 'the rector comes to lunch, and the Bishop one invites to dinner.' My mother reported this advice to my father, and when they had stopped laughing they agreed that the curate had been invited to dinner because he was much the most intelligent of the three.

Up to the year 1927 we used to visit Lady Gregory at Coole, travelling over from Ballylee in a pony and trap. It was always a thrill to make this trip, bumping along the narrow roads at what seemed enormous speed. My sister and I took turns to open the succession of gates along the long tree-lined drive into the Coole estate. I remember little about these visits, nor about Lady Gregory herself, save as a sort of brooding and formidable presence. As usual we were looked after by our nurse, but I did have one unwitting confrontation with Lady Gregory. She saw me eating the boiled potatoes, skins and all, and told me that I should peel them before eating them. Ever law-abiding, I did so, piling the skins neatly on the edge of the plate; and having eaten the potatoes, I then ate the skins (mine not to reason why!).

Just a few yards from the corner of the house there was a pump, used to supply water from the lake about a quarter of a mile away; it was worked (literally) by horse power. Thus every time I had a bath I could watch beforehand the horse going round and round attached to a pole that actuated the pumping system that sent the water up to the top of the house. This lake water was always brown, and I used to object to being given a bath in water that was already dirty.

In later years both Coole House and the tower at Ballylee were abandoned. After Lady Gregory's death the big house was empty for a while, and then was sold by the Land Commission to a builder in Galway, who demolished it in order to use the walls as building materials. This was during the years when tourism had not yet been thought of. Nowadays the grounds have been opened to visitors: the walled garden has been restored, but the house, alas, is gone for ever.

The tower at Ballylee has had a better fate. The cottages soon fell into ruin, but the massive stone tower itself still remained. Year by year, however, things disappeared: first the windows, then the floorboards, then the ceilings and the wooden joists, then the great wooden entrance door. At some stage various items of furniture began to disappear. One local man went off with a heavy full-length mirror – to preserve it from harm, of course – and was half-way home with it when he tired of carrying it. He therefore left it in a ditch by the side of the road, intending to come in the morning for it with a horse and cart. Later in the evening a local man who had had too much to drink staggered by (it was a moonlit night), saw himself reflected in the mirror and thought it was a ghost. He promptly took the pledge.

From the 1950s onwards my wife, Gráinne, and I would come to Ballylee each year and watch its gradual descent into ruin; we would lament that we ourselves would never be able to afford to restore it. One year to our amazement the ground floor of the tower was largely filled by a very large horse carriage. It must have been taken to pieces outside, brought through the narrow doorway, and then re-erected inside. The next time we came, it had disappeared.

After a long and very energetic campaign by Mary Hanley of Limerick and the local Kiltartan Society, Bord Fáilte were persuaded to restore the tower and thatched cottages, and open them to tourists. The whole place is a great deal warmer and more comfortable than ever it was in our day, but it still retains the romantic atmosphere that so appealed to my father.

At School

In 1927 the family visits to Ballylee and Coole came to an end. My father, who was by then 62 years old and in increasingly poor health, must have found the damp conditions at Ballylee difficult. He had been told by his doctors to avoid damp, and to spend part of the year in a warmer climate, so my parents rented a flat in the Italian seaside resort of Rapallo. This town was chosen because Ezra Pound lived there, the American poet who was closely connected with my parents and had been best man at their wedding.

In the same year, I was sent to a school in Switzerland called 'L'Alpe Fleurie', in Villars-sur-Bex. There I spent three years (1927–1930). I was told that I was sent there 'for my health', but I have never learned just what form this ill-health took: my mother always spoke vaguely of 'tubercular glands'. All I remember about the immediate illness is that I was placed in a nursing home in London, and was there dealt with by an amiable doctor who delighted me by producing a huge jar of boiled sweets, instructing me that I must eat these as rapidly as possible. Then after a while I was told that I was to go to a place where there were great big mountains. So in due course I was shipped off to a spot over 4,000 feet high, and to a school with an elaborate health programme involving much lying out in the sun on recliners, and prolonged periods in baths filled with a brown-coloured, strange smelling substance.

The school was housed in a large wooden chalet, perched on a slope overlooking the Rhone Valley and facing the 10,000-foot-high 'Dent du Midi'. The other boys and girls, varying widely in age and all presumably there for their health, were of various nationalities, but the language of the school was French, and it was forbidden to speak any other language. This could have caused problems for a six-year old boy, who could speak only

English, but to ensure my survival I was given one French word on my first day there – 'encore'. At least this would ensure that I was adequately fed. But in fact by the time I had been there six months I had become bilingual, and in time had perfect French. When after three years I came back to Ireland, I knew more French than English. After that, through lack of practice, I forgot nearly all my French, though my mother did her best to try to maintain it, bringing me to functions at the Alliance Française in Dublin. But the language was always there in the background; I could read or understand it without much difficulty, but it was many years later that circumstances compelled me to learn again to speak French – to find, however, that I had lost my once perfect French accent.

One might have expected that I would be lonely, suddenly thrown at the age of six amongst total strangers speaking strange languages, nearly a thousand miles from home. Yet I don't think I was, for to a small child distance means nothing. I was not at home, one mile or one thousand, it was all the same to me. One unpleasant aspect of this Swiss school was the constant occurrence of sometimes violent thunderstorms, particularly in summer. I had never known anything like these in Ireland, and I was frightened because the school building was made of wood, and I felt that any minute the place might go on fire.

But other things were pleasant enough. The snow in winter was – at first anyway – a new and interesting phenomenon. There were winter sports, of course. The older children went skiing, but I never graduated beyond ice skating: we used the skating rink attached to the large Villars Palace Hotel that was across the road from us. I never developed any elegance of style, but was able to skate at a high speed; unfortunately I was often unable to stop, and I once hurtled through a demonstration of figure skating, scattering dancers and audience on my way.

In the non-snow seasons we went on walks through the woods and fields in the neighbourhood, collecting bilberries when they were ripe. I soon grew tired of the scenery around Villars, especially the great white-topped mountain across the valley. Returning to the scene very many years later I realised that the whole area was indeed most beautiful. I suppose my childhood boredom with the scenery was an example of the old adage that 'you can't live on a view'.

After I had been in Switzerland for six months or so, my sister, Anne, arrived. There was nothing wrong with her health, but my mother presumably thought we would be company for each other. In the event, since she was two and a half years older than I was, we saw little of each other at the school. She was taught in different classes, indulged in different activities (such as skiing) and slept in a different part of the building.

We spent our Christmas holidays each year in Rapallo, in the flat that we had rented at the top of a six-story building. It was a long climb up the 82 steps, but there was also a lift, with a curious sign on it saying it was forbidden to use it for going down (my father had a special dispensation allowing him to use it in both directions). I saw more of my father in Rapallo than I had in earlier years, and we used to go down with him to bathe at the beach. He could swim very well under water, and was always willing to demonstrate this in order to amuse us.

It was probably in Rapallo that my mother embarked on a long campaign to get us to know him better, and to involve him in our lives. Unfortunately, one of her first efforts, when I was aged about seven, was to persuade him to teach me the game of chess. So he brought me out to one of the cafés on the sea-front, where there were table-tops marked out in squares. However, the occasion was a disaster, as I invented new rules whenever it seemed necessary; my father went home mentally exhausted, and spent the next two days in bed.

After coming back to Dublin from Switzerland in 1930, I had a governess for a while, and then I spent a year or so in a day school in Palmerston Park. I remember nothing whatever about this place, save for the daily electric tram journey to and fro. Instead of taking the tram from St Stephen's Green, near the flat in Fitzwilliam Square where we now lived, one could take the longish walk to a point where the tram fare changed. The saving by doing this was one penny each way, just enough for me to buy a favourite chocolate bar. There was a slight question of conscience, as to whether it was legitimate to divert my transport funds in this way, but after a short battle my conscience lost.

It was now that for the first time (as a 10 year old) I began to learn something about my own City of Dublin. My mother, as she admitted to me years later, embarked on a training course to ensure that when I grew up I would not be as helpless as my father was in dealing with the ordinary requirements of day-to-day living. When he was away in London or elsewhere she was liable to get telegrams from him asking, for example, 'Dining with so-and-so tomorrow. What do I wear?' She would send a telegram in reply saying 'Black tie' or whatever else was needed.

As part of my mother's training course she would send me out by myself to go for walks through the city streets. While I was still inexperienced, she would limit very severely the number of streets I could cross, but progressively, as she was satisfied that I was able to look after myself, the number of allowed crossings went up. In time I was able to range far and wide throughout the city, not only on foot, but also by the extensive tram system that I explored with enthusiasm, travelling from end to end on every single line.

This was the period when Dublin was notorious for its slums, in which whole families often lived in a single room – conditions sometimes compared with those in Calcutta. With my comfortable middle-class background I had never been exposed to conditions such as these, but now I would go walking through some of the poorer city areas, with half-ruined buildings everywhere, the children dressed in ragged clothing and running around barefoot. At the age of ten one does not embark on a crusade, and it did not occur to me that matters could (or even should) be changed. But I have no doubt that as the years went by my thinking on social matters was much affected by these early memories of Dublin poverty. For the first time I had learned that in the world there were the 'haves' and the 'have-nots'.

Before long, however, I was again launched into the rarified atmosphere of a boarding school. My mother had been looking for a school for me in Dublin, but the poet chose the occasion to write an imaginary letter to a schoolmaster. I should be taught Greek at once, he wrote, so that as I grew older I could read him the Greek lyric poets and he would talk to me about Plato. I was to be taught no Latin, geography, history or science. As regards mathematics, I was to be taught that subject as thoroughly as my capacity permitted. 'I know,' he wrote, 'that Bertrand Russell must, seeing that he is such a featherhead, be wrong about everything but as I have no mathematics I cannot prove it. I do not want my son to be so helpless.' I don't suppose any of this was meant to be taken seriously, but it was hardly a useful contribution when an important family decision had to be taken.

The school my mother chose for me was Baymount in Dollymount, a Dublin suburb, where around 30 boys were housed in Baymount Castle, a castellated building of nineteenth-century lineage. It was owned by W.L. (Bill) Scott, who acted as headmaster. I remember him mainly because he taught Latin and engendered in me a dislike for that language that has lasted ever since. He was in no sense a tyrant, and was in fact quite a nice man, but his concept of teaching was to present us on our very first day with 50 irregular verbs to learn.

There were other lists that we learned at Baymount. Each week a list of 200 difficult English words was placed on a notice board, to be learned by everyone by the end of the week. The best spellers were put onto the school team, which three times a year joined in competition with several hundred schools in Britain. There was much competition to get on the team, and I became a member quite soon. We were very successful, and gained first place overall term after term. The one permanent thing I gained from my three years at Baymount was an ability to spell.

I don't think I created any real impression at this school. I did well enough at the school work, beginning a long tradition in which my mother would complain about my School Reports. She would point to where some teacher would write 'could do better' or some such remark, I would counter by stressing the relative excellence of my examination results. The only occasions on which I was the source of much admiration from my fellow-pupils were on the daily walks, when we would set off round the neighbourhood in a long line. To while away the tedium of these walks, I took to telling the stories, in great detail, of such films as I had seen during the last holidays. To my surprise, these stories were a big hit, and I was much in demand as a sort of resident story-teller.

Just across the road from the school was the extensive St Anne's Estate – now a housing estate and public park – and we used to walk through this every Sunday on our way to Morning Service at St Anne's Church, Raheny. On the Estate was an enormous Georgian house (long since burnt down) inhabited by the retired Bishop Plunket, formerly Church of Ireland Bishop of Galway, who was reputedly worth millions. Living in the house also was his great-aunt, a venerable lady who was born in the same year (1821) as Queen Victoria, and had played with her as a child. We used to see her come to church every Sunday, the last occasion being just before she died at 112 years of age. Her only obvious concession to the advancing years was that she carried a cushion with her each week to place on the hard pew.

At Baymount we were considered to be the sons of gentlemen, and Bill Scott apparently felt he should inculcate in us the standards expected of our class. He told us a story once about how, as a young man, he had been in the company of a group of labouring men (his term), who were indulging in a variety of swear-words. In the course of his conversation with them he himself made use of a four-letter word – which he named for us – but was strongly reproved by his companions. It was all right for them, they said, to use such words, but for him (as a gentleman) it was quite wrong, and he should never do it. The complex social and class implications of this tale were quite above our childish heads, particularly since we had never heard this word and had no idea what it meant. In these democratic days, of course, as we approach the Millennium, the social differences between the swearers and the non-swearers are by no means so clear-cut.

Being the sons of Protestant gentlemen meant that they were all very pro-British – and the teachers also. The boys had no interest whatever in politics, but had gained their outlook from their parents and from their general family background. The 'Anglo-Irish' of that day were still trying to come to terms with the new Ireland. They were gradually coming to accept that the Unionist days were over, but their eyes were still pointed firmly towards Britain.

The boys at Baymount would in almost all cases go on later to an English public school. Most of them would take up careers in the Army (British of course) or other positions in Britain or in the Empire on which the sun still never set. Their families listened reverently to the King's speech on the BBC at Christmas. In church on Remembrance Day and on other occasions when it seemed expedient, they would raise their voices in song, calling on the Almighty to look after the King of England: 'send him victorious, long to reign over us, happy and glorious, God save the King.' Their only source of news about Ireland was *The Irish Times*, still staunchly Unionist, with its daily Court and Personal column faithfully retailing the then respectable comings and goings of the various members of the Royal Family. At election time they voted for the Cumann na nGaedheal Government, not because they had any particular liking for William Cosgrave, but because he wanted to retain whatever ties with Britain remained after the Treaty. In any event, he was greatly to be preferred to Eamon de Valera, who was considered to be a dangerous republican who stood for everything that the 'Anglo-Irish' of the day feared and hated.

I myself, on the other hand, came from a totally different family background. My grandfather, the portrait painter John Butler Yeats, had abandoned the traditional Unionism of his family, and in due course handed on his Home Rule principles to his children. My father, however, adopted a much more radical form of nationalism under the influence of the old Fenian John O'Leary. For many years he used his influence as a poet in the national struggle; he supported the 1921 Treaty, unlike my uncle Jack Yeats, who took the other side. But I knew none of all this; nor did I know until years later that my mother supported Fianna Fáil. My parents used to discuss at election-time whether it was worth going to the polls, since they would cancel each other out, but in the end would decide that it was their civic duty to vote. Politics, or public issues in general, had never been discussed in my hearing at home. Perhaps it was felt such topics were unsuitable for a child, or else that I would be bored: if the latter was their reason, then they were wrong.

In any event I arrived at Baymount School knowing nothing about the great events that were taking place outside its walls. The country during the early 1930s was in a fever of political activity, with a new Fianna Fáil Government under Eamon de Valera, the abolition of the Oath of Allegiance, the Economic War with Britain, the formation of the semi-Fascist Blueshirt movement with which for a brief period my father was involved. Of all this I knew nothing – I did not even at that time know that my father had been a Senator. I had never heard of Cosgrave or de Valera. There was just one thing I did know. I knew that I was Irish and that I felt no sense of loyalty to any other country. But so far as politics was concerned, my mind was a blank, open to influence from any source.

It soon became clear to me that everyone else in the school held one fixed view. Not quite appreciating the nuances of their parents' political party attitudes, the boys all proclaimed that Cosgrave must be supported because – he might have been surprised to hear – he was pro-British. De Valera, on the other hand, was to be condemned on numerous grounds, most particularly because he wanted to break away completely from Britain and to establish an Irish Republic. Surrounded by these vociferously stated views, I had to make a decision for myself. As presented to me, this was an issue to which there could only be one clear and common-sense answer. By the time I left Baymount School at the age of 14, I had become a committed de Valera republican.

Border Politics

After my period at Baymount School, a decision had to be made as to where I would go next, and my father once more entered the field. He announced with enthusiasm that he had discovered an ideal school for me near Oxford, where all the work was done through the medium of Greek. Since I had never been taught any Greek this would have presented me with something of a problem. However in the Yeats household such decisions were fortunately taken by my mother, and she had long since decided that I should go to St Columba's College. This Church of Ireland school, perched on the side of Two Rock Mountain, was just 3 miles from Rathfarnham, the suburb of Dublin where we now lived.

Before I actually arrived at St Columba's, my parents paid an official visit to see the school, and were shown around the premises by the Warden (headmaster), and Vice-Warden. As they walked round, my father began a stiff cross-examination of the Warden, Rev. C.W. Sowby, demanding to be given a detailed explanation of the state of the College drains – about which the Warden in fact probably knew very little. When my parents got home, my mother asked 'Willy, why on earth did you choose the College drains as a suitable subject for inquiry?' 'Well', he said, 'you told me to behave like a father and to show an interest in the school, and I couldn't think of any other subject to discuss.'

St Columba's was founded in 1843. At that time most of the boys were the sons of landlords, and they were taught the Irish language so that they could talk to their tenants, many of whom could not speak English. The College was intended to be an Irish version of a British 'public school', that system designed to create a ruling class that would build and govern the empire. Even a century later, St Columba's still retained most of the characteristics of that peculiar British institution. There was a general lack of comfort. The classrooms were heated, but the dormitories were not, so that we were really cold on winter nights, 500 feet up on the mountainside. We had to take a cold bath every morning, for some reason never explained.

In accordance with the practice in British public schools, there was corporal punishment, which could be carried out not only by the masters, but also by those boys who had been appointed prefects. It took the form of two, four, or six strokes on the bottom with a cane. I only suffered from this once, when the warden gave me four strokes for the heinous offence of borrowing someone else's games clothes. I didn't find the punishment particularly painful, and I don't think that those with greater experience than I worried unduly about their beatings.

The prefects were appointed by the Warden from amongst the most senior boys. They played a general role in maintaining discipline, and one of them each evening would preside over the homework period in the big schoolroom. These prefects were often bullies. They had their own common room, and operated a 'fagging' system. All the junior boys were 'fags', and had to carry out any tasks imposed on them by the prefects. At frequent intervals there would come from the prefects' common room a loud shout of 'fag!' and then we juniors all had to run to the room. The last to arrive was given the task to perform, getting the prefect a cup of water, or whatever.

The boys, as at my previous school, had the typical prejudices of the 'Anglo-Irish' of the day and were therefore pro-British and pro-Cosgrave. There was also a small contingent of boys from Northern Ireland, who were, of course, out-and-out Unionists. One of these was Brian Faulkner, who was my greatest friend at St Columba's and for a number of years afterwards. Poppies were worn on Armistice Day, we were exposed to broadcasts by British royalty, there was much talk of 'The Army'. Some of the masters were Irish with the usual 'Anglo-Irish' politics, others were English, and one or two of the latter were inclined to support Fianna Fáil in a mild way, perhaps because they supported the Labour Party in England and their political attitudes were therefore more radical. A real 'odd man out' amongst the masters was George Lodge, the main Science teacher, who was a Catholic, and according to legend had driven the taxi that brought Eamon de Valera to safety when he escaped in 1920 from Lincoln Jail. I don't know whether there was any truth in this, but it made him in our eyes a vaguely romantic figure. He had been at the College from time immemorial, and I often wondered how such a normal Irishman had been hired in the first place.

The efforts of St Columba's to ape the British public school system were in fact less than successful, perhaps because Irish boys were not so willing to conform. Whatever the reason, the College tolerated, even encouraged, eccentricity. The boys were allowed to keep pets in various sheds about the place, not the usual domestic pets, but such animals as ferrets, hawks, goats and so on. The hawks were acquired young, and were trained to hunt. This involved, of course, feeding them with rodents, small rabbits and other such animals, so that they would get the idea and in time go foraging for themselves. To acquire these small titbits their owners would go walking over the mountains with a shotgun, a weapon that even St Columba's would normally have banned. But when the Vice-Warden met one of these shotgun carrying youths on the mountainside one day, he was at pains not to notice the gun. He realised, apparently, that hawks had to be fed.

There was another boy who had a passion for explosives. He would dig a hole in a field and put dynamite in it, cover it up and then retreat to the edge of the field. When set off with a fuse, the dynamite made a very satisfactory explosion. There was no political intent in all this, he just liked the noise.

The Rev. C.W. Sowby, the Warden of the College was despised by the students – even the most Unionist amongst us – because he was so very English. These boys might be pro-British, but they had a healthy contempt for the English, an attitude still often held today in Northern Ireland, even by the likes of Ian Paisley. Like many English people who work abroad, Sowby had all the instinct of the chameleon, ever anxious to ape the manners and habits of the locals; but of course he never came near succeeding. Trying to inculcate in us the 'stiff-upper-lip' attitudes of his countrymen, he told us once a story about a city in some part of the far-flung Empire. It seems that there was a tremendous downpour of rain, so much so that all traffic stopped and, he said, the policeman on point duty – there being no traffic to direct – sought shelter in a nearby doorway. An

Englishman would not have done this, but would have stayed on at his post no matter what. We thought this was idiotic, so the effect on us of the Warden's little moral tale was quite the opposite of what he had intended.

We had a sister-school in England, called Radley, and once a year a half-dozen boys from there would come over to spend a week with us. They would of course be shown around the neighbourhood, and a favourite ploy was to bring them across some field and then say suddenly in alarmed tones that armed men were drilling in an adjoining field. 'Quick, down in the ditch,' we would say, and they would be brought crawling through the mud until we told them that it was safe to emerge. Amongst the most active in this would be Unionists such as Brian Faulkner.

While at the college I maintained and strengthened my support for de Valera and Fianna Fáil. There were newspapers available in College (even if only the Unionist *Irish Times*), and I naturally developed an increasing interest in public affairs. I had endless arguments with the other boys, especially at election time. During the 1937 General Election count, the proceedings adjourned with Fianna Fáil ahead in seats, and I exulted greatly over all concerned. In later years I became an expert on the Proportional Representation (PR) system of election, but I was no expert then. Next day the final result of the election was 69-69, and in their turn they all exulted over me. But I got my own back next year, when Fianna Fáil got an overall majority of 16 in the 1938 election.

Party politics was not the only national issue about which I was in the minority. This was the period of the first great drive to manufacture goods in Ireland, and an accompanying campaign to persuade people to buy them. For many years after the drive began there was a feeling (sometimes justified) that Irish-made goods were inferior. When we began playing hockey at the college I acquired a new stick – made of course in Ireland – and was laughed at by a classmate who himself had what he claimed to be a much better English-made one. My joy was great when, half an hour later, his own stick broke in half.

Of course it was not just the West British element who had this attitude. It was very difficult in those early days to persuade the public in general to buy Irish. In the early 1930s the well-known Sunlight soap, formerly made by Unilever in Liverpool, began to be manufactured in Ireland, The new factory was opened with much publicity by Seán Lemass, who told me years later what happened. For the first three months after the factory opened, there was an immense stream of angry letters from all over Ireland, with bitter complaints about the wretched quality of the soap. Why, oh why, was the constant refrain, could they not go back to the good old days when the soap was made in England? The strange thing, Lemass said, was that during those three months the Dublin factory was still selling off their old English stock. Not one single bar of Irish-made soap had yet been put on the market.

It follows from all this that I was in a minority of one at St Columba's, just as I had been at my previous school. Had I been good at games I might perhaps have been accepted as a normal member of society, but in fact at rugby football, hockey and cricket I was hopeless, and therefore was scorned by those athletic types who are inevitably dominant in all boys' schools.

My position was made more difficult by the fact that my father was a poet. At least that in itself might not have mattered, but unfortunately I had just come to the College when someone discovered the Yeats poem called 'A Prayer for my Son'. When my sister, Anne, was born, there appeared 'A Prayer for my Daughter', which is a fine poem, whatever complaints people may have about the political sentiments expressed in it. When I in due course appeared, my father apparently felt that in all fairness he should also produce a poem for me, but unfortunately he celebrated my birth in verse of maudlin sentimentality:

> *Bid a strong ghost stand at the head*
> *That my Michael may sleep sound,*
> *Nor cry, nor turn in the bed*
> *Till his morning meal come round.*

It is not surprising that my fellows at the College should have been overjoyed to come across this. Once it was understood that the recitation of these lines was sufficient to enrage me, then the word was passed around and everyone joined in the game. In due course, to save time and trouble, the quotation was cut down to 'Bid a strong ghost', and finally the initials

BASG were all that was needed to drive me into a fury. My advice to poets ever since has been, if you must write poems about your children, do not publish them until they have left school.

It was always a surprise to people that Brian Faulkner and I should have become inseparable friends, almost from our first arrival at St Columba's in September, 1935. I was tall and he was short (we were often referred to as Mutt and Jeff), we stemmed from entirely different backgrounds, our temperaments were different and, of course, our political and national attitudes were totally opposed. I was an Irish nationalist believing in total separation from Britain, he was a typical Northern Unionist.

It may be, however, that our differing attitudes on Irish issues helped to bring us together. I have always been passionately addicted to political debate, in which he in turn was happy to join. But there must have been other things that attracted us to each other. I can only conclude that there was something in our respective characters that had a mutual appeal, and thus we maintained a friendship that lasted through our school days and for a number of years afterwards.

Brian Faulkner was the first Northern Unionist I had ever met, and his political attitudes were poles apart from the pallid West-British atmosphere that I had grown used to at Baymount School and now again at St Columba's. These 'Southern Loyalists' professed to love Ireland, but could not envisage Ireland save as an integral part of the United Kingdom and the British Empire. Brian, on the other hand, centered all his loyalties on the Six counties. He was typical of his fellow Unionists in their wish to remain part of Britain, but strictly on their own terms. At the age of 14 he had no interest at all in party politics: to him, politicians were people who replaced action by talk. He sneered at the British Parliament in London, and laughed at the Orange Order.

He was not anti-Catholic in any sort of bigoted way. By this I mean that I never heard him insult or criticise anyone's religion – there were no remarks about 'papists' in the style of the Orange Order or of the Paisleyites today. But he had all the usual Unionist attitudes about the Northern minority. They were lazy, feckless and untidy, and you could always tell a Catholic house or farm by its unkempt appearance. When I would attack him – as I often did – about the gerrymandering, the constant discrimination against the minority in jobs, housing and many other fields, he would justify these on the specious grounds that they only existed because the minority were 'disloyal'. In other words, if the Catholics accepted the Oath of Allegiance and reconciled themselves to their permanent exclusion from the rest of Ireland, then it would be possible to end the various forms of discrimination against them.

Not surprisingly we argued endlessly about such issues, both at school and during our frequent visits to each other during the holidays. Much of this was on a decidedly juvenile plane. Thus Brian would bring me to see the Stormont Parliament building; I would duly admire it, adding that some day it would make a fine museum. Or he would boast of the new trolley-bus system recently installed in Belfast – Dublin having nothing better than old electric trams. Those were the days when Dún Laoghaire was never referred to as such by the old-style West British, so when we were on a tram one day, Brian rushed in ahead of me to ask the conductor for 'two to Kingstown'. To my delight he replied that there was no such place on the line. Even when we had left school and should by now have acquired more adult patterns of behaviour, this sort of thing continued. Brian wrote to me one day, addressing the letter to the Irish Free State; so I sent my reply to Comber, Co. Down, Éire. Nothing was ever said, but future letters carried, as usual, addresses ending with Dublin and Co. Down respectively.

Occasionally we went on trips together, such as a cycle ride we took in the West of Ireland, mainly staying at youth hostels. We took the train to Galway, and from there went round the coast, ending up in Achill Island. On the way we ran into a period of very bad weather, so for two days we retreated to be looked after by the nuns at their guest house at Kylemore Abbey. I told Brian that his friends and acquaintances would be shocked by his staying in a convent. It was on this trip, cycling through Louisburgh, Co. Mayo, that we saw a happening that has puzzled me ever since. As we passed by a terrace of prosperous, middle-class houses, the front door of one opened, and down the front steps came a sleek and well-fed cow. After the cow came a priest. When they reached the pavement, the cow set off in one direction, the priest in the other. I have never been able to think of an even remotely rational explanation for this curious event.

Another time we toured Co. Cork, this time by train and bus, and we were walking down Patrick Street in Cork City when a loud voice hailed me from across the street. It was that well-known Cork man Eoin O'Mahony – universally known as 'the Pope'. I introduced him to Brian Faulkner, and Eoin asked him what he would like to see. So Brian suggested Sunbeam Wolsey (the biggest textile factory in the City). 'No problem at all', said O'Mahony, 'the owner of the factory, Billy Dwyer, is an old friend of mine, and he will be delighted to see us.' But when we got there the atmosphere seemed a bit cool, and after some 40 minutes an infuriated William Dwyer appeared, flanked by his son Declan. They took Eoin outside and for about ten minutes they yelled at him, with much bad language. In the end we were flung out of the place, and as we walked up the long drive leading to the street, the Dwyers continued roaring at us until we had gone out of sight. It turned out that at the General Election just three weeks before, William Dwyer had stood for the Opposition Fine Gael party and did so badly that he lost his deposit. It had been one of the dirtiest elections in Cork history and Eoin O'Mahony, then with Fianna Fáil, had been one of the most active in flinging mud. It was typical of Eoin that in three weeks he had already forgotten all this, and had assumed that everyone else had forgotten also.

At one stage during the war years Brian got himself a motor bike; there was far more petrol available in the North than across the Border. Being 'young and foolish' I enjoyed gadding about on this machine, and from the pillion seat would urge him on to ever greater speeds. We used to race the passenger trains that ran for some distance alongside the road from Belfast to Comber. At the point where the road and the railway line diverged, we and the engine driver would exchange waves.

Brian's father was James A. Faulkner, who owned a large shirt factory in West Belfast; about one thousand girls worked there. The factory had acquired the first conveyor belt in Ireland, which was installed by a German expert from Berlin. When he presented his account, for £400, Faulkner Senior said he thought it was too high. 'Ah', the German said, 'that is £100 for my work, and £300 for knowing how.' But in fact James Faulkner and his factory manager had kept a good eye on what the expert was doing, and the next time a conveyor belt was needed they put it in themselves. We often visited the factory, and I used to watch what must have been soul-destroying work on the conveyor belts. Each girl would spend the entire day on a single task – for example, sewing on the third button from the top on each shirt as it went by. In fact they didn't seem to mind, and appeared always to be engaged in cheerful conversation. The manager of the shirt factory (who was on a British Army reserve) was called up at the start of the War, so Brian, who had been studying Law in Queen's University, and was not yet 19, had to take over the running of the business.

For most of the time we were at school the Faulkners lived in Bangor, but they then moved to a 60-acre farm near Comber, Co. Down. They carried on farming operations on a fairly intensive scale, with more machinery than was customary in those days – all this had to be removed from the fields each Saturday night, in case any of their Protestant neighbours would think that they were working on the Sabbath.

The Faulkner family were receptive to new ideas, including the rather odd concept that plants of all kinds would grow faster if the seed was planted at the time of the full moon. They showed me a pamphlet in which the evidence for this was set out in detail, with numerous photographs of plants, showing the much superior development of those planted at the right lunar period. It all seemed quite plausible, but reason suggests, some 50 years later, that if there was anything in it the farmers of the world would long since have regulated their planting operations by the light of the moon.

I was staying with the Faulkners on their farm the night of the first big air raid on Belfast in 1941. Almost all night long, we could hear the sinister drone of the stream of Junker bombers flying overhead. Early next morning we drove the 15 miles into the City to see how things were, and in particular to see whether the shirt factory had been damaged. It had not, though there had been great damage in other places and a large number of dead. Here and there we saw the fire engines that had come up during the night from Dundalk, Drogheda, Dublin and other towns south of the Border. That was one of the few occasions on which all Ireland really became one. When the magnitude of the emergency became clear, the Belfast authorities rang Dublin to ask for help. De Valera was woken in the middle of the night and said instantly that all possible aid should be sent. Neutrality was not an issue when any part of Ireland needed help.

It was from Brian Faulkner that I learned that the Unionist majority in Northern Ireland was by no means as monolithic as appearances suggested; this was the period when the Unionist Party regularly got the support of almost the entire Protestant vote. Brian often used to talk about the old days, when his Presbyterian Church was discriminated against by the then established Church of Ireland. As we drove or cycled through the villages of Co. Down, he would point to the Church of Ireland building in the best site on the top of a hill, and then to the Presbyterian church that was always in a much inferior place. Later on, as he himself developed an interest in party politics, he extended these criticisms to cover the Unionist Party. Ever since Stormont was set up, he pointed out, the party had been led by members of the Church of Ireland landowning class, first Craigavon, then John Andrews, then Lord Brookeborough.

In later years it was under Lord Brookeborough that Brian himself entered politics. In a party of nonentities his rise was rapid and he became an extremely efficient Minister for Commerce. But Lord Brookeborough in due course was succeeded by Terence O'Neill, who was well-meaning but ineffectual, and he in turn arranged to be succeeded by yet another mediocrity from the landowning class, Chichester-Clarke, who in the Party election beat Brian Faulkner by one vote. This long period of weak leadership by politicians who no longer had the trust of large elements of the Unionist population, created the conditions leading to the rise of Ian Paisley.

After Chichester-Clarke, Brian Faulkner could not be kept out any longer, and he became the first Stormont Prime Minister from the middle-class business community, and a Presbyterian at that. I have wondered sometimes what would have happened if he had been selected, for example, to succeed Lord Brookeborough. It is possible that he could have held together the old monolithic Unionist Party for at least some years longer.

It was the tragedy of Unionism in the North that, while Brian Faulkner's attitudes remained essentially the same, with the coming of Paisley and his ilk the mainstream of Unionist thinking moved sharply to the right. The Faulkner who had been so much condemned as a hard-liner did not really change, but ended up being spoken of as a liberal. He was always a pragmatist, and during the Sunningdale negotiations he in the end accepted the principle of power sharing, not because he liked the idea but because it had become inevitable. Uncharacteristically, however, he also accepted the creation of an All-Ireland Parliamentary Council, though he certainly should have known that such a Council would not at that time be accepted by his Unionist Party.

In the brief period, however, that the Unionist/SDLP Government lasted, there did, I think, come about a change in Brian Faulkner's attitude to power sharing. His first reaction seems to have been one of deep suspicion, though in keeping with his pragmatic approach to life it is likely that, having been forced to accept this new approach, he decided to do his utmost to make it work. For his own political future, of course, it had to work. But as time went on it appears that he became genuinely enthusiastic about the working of the power-sharing Government. One of his former SDLP colleagues in Government painted for me a tragic picture of him weeping at the Cabinet table during the last meeting before it collapsed as a result of the Paisleyite strike.

It seems also that he told his SDLP colleagues that it was because of my influence that he originally decided to embark on a political career. We had spent a good eight years in a more or less constant discussion of Irish political issues, so that in the end he abandoned his contempt for politicians and became one himself. Even though he used to laugh at the Orange Order, since membership of that institution was essential for any Unionist parliamentarian, he joined the Order and wore the Sash with at least outward enthusiasm. Another preparation that he felt was necessary for a budding Unionist politician was to withdraw gradually from our friendship. There was no falling-out of any kind, but he apparently decided that a close friendship with a Fianna Fáil activist in Dublin was not in his best interests. While I perfectly understood his reasoning, I felt that (even from his narrow party point of view) his decision was not necessary. I always regretted that he should have allowed political ambition to interfere with the ties of a friendship of many years.

During all Brian Faulkner's political career he had the reputation of being a dour personality, and certainly in photographs he exuded a sort of tight-lipped gloom, with never a smile to be seen. I don't know whether he felt that this was the sort of persona expected of a 'statesman', but at any rate it conveyed a quite misleading impression of his real character. As I knew Brian, he was a cheerful person who got on very well with people, and had a good sense of humour. My memories of him are happy ones. For a number of years he meant a great deal to me, and I owed much to him. I was very sad when I heard of his sudden death as the result of a fall from a horse. Though I had seen him perhaps twice in the previous thirty years, his image was as fresh to me as if our friendship had continued without a break up to the moment of his death.

A Poet in the Family

My father died in January, 1939, while I was still at St Columba's College. He had been in ill health for many years, so that his death, though quite sudden, was not a surprise. While the loss of a parent is of course always a shock, I cannot say that I felt any deep sense of personal loss. He had always been for me a formidable, towering figure – in a way it was like living with a national monument. I did, however, regret very much that he should have gone just as I had begun to establish a closer relationship with him than I had ever had before.

My parents had gone to stay for the winter in a little hotel (Idéal Séjour) in Roquebrune on the French Riviera, and I went out from school to spend the Christmas holidays there. While my father was now physically very weak, mentally he was as lively as ever, and we had some animated discussions on the politics of central Europe. For me this was a revelation. The remote and distant figure of my childhood had been replaced by someone with whom I could talk on a basis of equality. It was during those few weeks in France that for the first time I had a serious conversation or discussion with him. My mother always maintained that he had no interest in people as such, only in what they said or did, and I suppose that at 17 I had at last reached a degree of maturity that made me interesting in his eyes. My sister, Anne, had in fact reached this status some time before. Not only was she older than I was, but her interests were those also of my father: she was an artist, and had for some years designed scenery for the Abbey Theatre. The two of them, therefore, had things about which they could talk.

The passing of a great poet, of course, is a matter of worldwide interest, and in the almost 60 years since my father's death there has been an endless stream of newspaper articles, essays and books about him. His life and his amazingly varied career have been discussed in detail, his writings have been analysed from every possible standpoint. But what in fact was he like? He was a man of many masks, and could project totally different images, depending on the person he was meeting or the circumstances of the time. That may be why many of the depictions of W.B. Yeats bear little relationship to the father we knew at home. To us he was certainly a remote figure, but even so we were able over the years to build our own picture of the poet in the family.

His own public image changed greatly with the years. There are photographs of him as a young man when he was acting the part of a poet – described by George Moore as having 'a long black cloak drooping from his shoulders, a soft black sombrero on his head, a voluminous black silk tie flowing from his collar, long black trousers dragging untidily over his long, heavy feet.' For this reason he is often portrayed as somewhat effete, with a languid manner and affected accent. By the 1930s all this had changed and a photograph of him making a radio broadcast shows him, in old age, full of vivacity and humour. This is the Yeats that I remember.

Far from speaking in an affected way, my father had a pronounced Sligo accent. He had a strong voice, and my mother said that when giving public lectures he was able to speak to audiences of 2,000 or more without amplification. At home, on occasions when he set out to amuse us children, he could be a most entertaining talker, with a strong, sometimes sardonic, sense of humour. I remember sitting at the dinner table listening to him, and wondering whether, when I grew up, I would be able to tell stories as well as he did.

I can remember just two little stories that he obviously intended specifically for Anne and myself. He told us that the poet Robert Browning boasted one day in his club that he could make a poem to rhyme with anything. One of the club members therefore challenged him to find a rhyme for 'Timbuktu', upon which Browning produced this epic:

There was a cassowary
in Timbuktu,
Who ate a missionary
and his hymn book too.

On another occasion my father told us children that in his youth in Sligo there was held in the locality a sausage-eating competition, to decide who could eat the most sausages in a five-minute period. The prize was to be an old-style fob watch – the sort that you kept in your pocket. The prize was won by a young fellow called Joe, who was delighted to receive the watch; the only problem was that he had never learned to read the time. So for the rest of his life, according to my father, whenever anyone asked him the time he would take out the watch and say 'My God, I didn't know it was so late,' and rush off into the distance.

However, telling us amusing stories was one thing, actually talking to us as individuals was quite another. My father simply had no idea how to talk to children. My mother decided that Anne, then aged about 14, should go into his study every day for half an hour after dinner, so that the two of them could get into conversation. Anne had no idea what she was supposed to say, but on the first evening she did her best to get a discussion going, with very little success. The next day things went equally badly. On the third day Anne decided she would have to do something about this, so she mentioned the name of the English poet and painter, Dante Gabriel Rossetti. My father thereupon embarked on a monologue which continued for the next half hour. That was the end of the experiment.

My father obviously thought highly of Dante Gabriel Rossetti, but that poet also had a younger brother, William Michael, a literary and art critic, who had a life-long effect on me. My parents had decided I should be called William Michael Butler, and my birth certificate includes these names. But my father then remembered that he disapproved of the younger Rossetti, and decreed that I could not bear the same names: so on my baptism the 'William' was dropped.

On another occasion my mother decided – in a further attempt to bring the poet closer to his children – that he should read to us. He obligingly did so, embarking on Walter Scott's 'Lay of the Last Minstrel'. We wondered why he chose to read this rather out-dated poem, until he explained that (more than 50 years earlier) his own father had read it to him. Other, more spontaneous, activities succeeded better.

The house (called 'Riversdale'), that we rented near Rathfarnham during the 1930s had a large garden, including a lawn on which croquet could be played. My father, in spite of bad eyesight and ill health, became a skilful and highly competitive player; so there was this one field at least, on which we could meet on something like free and easy terms. One afternoon a relative came visiting, and was immediately bidden to play croquet. Seeing only that my father was old and in poor health, she decided he needed help, and with her foot quietly pushed his ball into a better position. He saw her do this, and decreed that never again was she to be invited to play croquet.

Only once in all our childhood did my father get involved in family discipline. Neither Anne nor myself can remember just what we had done to deserve this unprecedented intervention, but presumably we had been quarrelling. At any rate he took us into a room, sat us down and recited a poem. He then left, leaving us bemused and somewhat over-awed by the solemnity of the occasion. This poem was an eighteenth-century one by Isaac Watts, and in later years we looked up the text given in the Oxford Book of Quotations. It runs:

Let dogs delight to bark and bite,
For God hath made them so;
Let bears and lions growl and fight,
For 'tis **their** *nature too.*

But, children, **you** *should never let*
Such angry passions rise;
Your *little hands were never made*
To tear each other's eyes.

Just once, my father made a decisive intervention in family affairs. Our parents had agreed that Anne, then a teenager, should join the Girl Guides, not realising, apparently, that at that time this was a thoroughly 'British' organisation. All went well for a few weeks until one Sunday a Church Parade was held, at which a Union Jack flag was raised with much solemnity. Anne duly reported this event at home, upon which the poet sent a severe letter to the Rev. O'Sullivan, the Church of Ireland Rector of Rathfarnham, demanding that the flag be removed at once. The flag thereupon disappeared, and was never seen again.

It was some 40 years later that we heard the inside story of the flag affair. My wife, Gráinne, and I were told by the Rev. Walter Burrowes, then Rector of Dundrum (who had baptised several of our children), that at the time of the affair he had been a young curate in Rathfarnham. It seemed that my father's letter created a most appalling problem, as the Union Jack had been especially presented to the Girl Guide troupe by a Mrs Shaw, who was by far the richest and most generous of the parishioners.

What was the Rector to do? Was he to risk the alienation of the generous Mrs Shaw, or should he defy the great poet, who might then attack him in letters to the newspapers, or hold a public meeting or, worst of all, write a poem about the affair, in which for centuries to come the infamy of the Rector and the parish would be set out for all to read? In the end the Rector went to see Mrs Shaw, who quite understood his problem, and agreed to take back her Union Jack.

This was not the only political controversy created during the seven years that we lived in Rathfarnham. Since we had the use of a large garden my mother was able to construct a hen-run, in which she kept around two dozen hens. One day her favourite white hen disappeared, and she immediately decided where lay the responsibility. Our next-door neighbours were a family called Weldon, of whom she particularly disapproved because they were members of the semi-Fascist 'Blueshirt' movement that was active for a brief period in the 1930s. These Weldons owned several mongrel dogs, and my mother was convinced that one of these had done away with her white hen.

She sent our gardener (John Free) round to the Weldons with a note of complaint, and a note came back claiming that their dogs were innocent. She therefore sent a further note, saying that she was going to complain to the Gardaí that the Weldons' dogs were clearly out of control – and most likely did not have a dog licence between them. A further reply then came back saying 'We have no dogs', and John Free confirmed that this was in fact true, as they had drowned all five of them. This upset my mother very much, since while she disliked the Weldons for purely political reasons, she had nothing in particular against the dogs. And she felt very much worse next day, when her white hen returned.

She fled to my father and sought his advice and, when he had stopped laughing, he said that on no account should she let the Weldons see that the hen still lived. She would have to kill it. 'But,' she said, 'that hen is my best layer!' He insisted, however, that there was no alternative, so on the following Sunday we had the white hen for dinner. Even such a small domestic event as this can be grist to a poet's mill, so a (1934) version of 'Three Songs to the Same Tune' includes a verse that reads:

> *'Drown all the dogs,' said the fierce young woman,*
> *'They killed my goose and a cat.*
> *Drown, drown in the water-butt,*
> *Drown all the dogs,' said the fierce young woman.*

A few years after this event, there was much discussion in the newspapers as to who would become the first President of Ireland after the adoption of the Constitution in 1937. One afternoon my father was visited by his old friend and collaborator Dr Douglas Hyde, who had just that morning been suggested by *The Irish Times* as a possible President. Hyde was not impressed: 'Now that *The Irish Times* has suggested my name,' he said, 'that ends any chance I might have had.' However, he did in fact become President in 1938, with the support of all the political parties.

In the months after he took office, Douglas Hyde would on occasion complain to my parents about life in Áras an Uachtaráin. It seemed that in those early days everything was organised in the most rigid civil service fashion; if the President wanted to pick a peach in the Áras greenhouse, he had first to get the permission of the Board of Works. Even, Hyde said plaintively, when he tried to poke his own coal fire, there was always someone who would insist on doing it for him.

We in the family – and everybody who knew him – realised my father's combination of a man of action with one afflicted by extreme absent-mindedness. When political or national affairs were in question he was a highly effective operator, delighting in controversy. He was always business-like in dealing with the affairs of the Abbey Theatre, or when negotiating with publishers. He was also careful about money: in this he was probably influenced by memories of his father John Butler Yeats who, though at his best a fine portrait painter, was incapable of making money, or of keeping it once made. When in 1923 he won the Nobel Prize for Literature, R.M. Smyllie of *The Irish Times* rang him up to tell him the news. Smyllie was in the midst of a speech saying what a great day this was for Ireland, when my father broke in to ask, 'How much, Smyllie, how much?' (the answer was £7,500).

At other times he could be astonishingly absent-minded, as on the well-documented occasion when, having had dinner at the Arts Club in Dublin, he was so absorbed in conversation that when told he had not yet eaten he believed this, and went in and had a second dinner. One evening, when we were still in Merrion Square, my parents had a guest for dinner. My mother brought in a roast chicken and put it on the table, and then headed again for the kitchen. When she returned a few minutes later with a dish of vegetables, she found my father and the guest in avid conversation, and between them the family cat busy eating the chicken. She did not at all appreciate the humour of this, and when she told me the tale, years later, her voice was still filled with indignation.

My mother told me of another occasion when the poet got so absorbed in the conversation at dinner that he did not notice what he was eating. This was one of those very formal public affairs – probably in England – with a footman behind each guest. Along with the main course my father was offered parsnips, which he refused, since this was a vegetable that he very much disliked. Some time later, while he was involved in a particularly interesting discussion, another waiter came along and placed a pile of parsnips on his plate. He ate this, and then turned to my mother and said 'George, that wasn't a very nice pudding.'

On one occasion in the 1920s our house in Merrion Square was briefly in the public eye. We lived at No. 82, and my father's great friend George Russell ('AE'), the poet and mystic, lived at No. 84. They were both very absent-minded, and one afternoon they set off simultaneously to visit each other. Russell as usual walked with his hands behind his back and his head down, my father with his hands behind his back and his head in the air. They passed each other on the pavement, and knocked on each other's door. By chance a well-known cartoonist of the day, Isa McNee, was just across the street at this moment, and the humorous journal *Dublin Opinion* appeared the following week with a cartoon by her illustrating this event.

My father, when he was in sufficiently good health, would have regular working periods in his study, during which childish noise was supposed to be kept to a minimum. He was a very slow worker, and his manuscripts show that in the case even of a short poem there would be a series of false starts, deletions and amendments. The whole process of composition was infinitely laborious, and it is not surprising that he considered four or five lines of poetry to be a good day's work. Once he felt that a poem was finished he would dictate it to my mother, who acted as his secretary. Even while she was typing out the poem he would look over her shoulder and make further amendments, so that there might be a half-dozen or more versions typed and corrected before he was satisfied.

Partly because of his poor eyesight, his writing was almost impossible to read. This was made even more difficult by a total inability to spell even simple words correctly ('gas' would be spelt 'gass'). His punctuation, also, was peculiar. It was not merely, my mother said, that he did not understand punctuation: in poetry, he did not use it at all. When dictating prose to her, on the other hand, he would put in a stop or dash every time he paused for thought. Where thought was not needed, things were different. Once as he dictated a prose passage, after three-quarters of an hour he suddenly said, 'Comma'.

Apart from his regular periods of work, my father might begin the process of composition at any time. All the family knew the signs, we were careful to do nothing that might interrupt the flow of thought. Without warning he would begin to make a low, tuneless humming sound, and his right hand would wave vaguely as if beating time. This could happen at the dinner table, while playing croquet, or sitting in a bus, and he would become totally oblivious to what was going on around him. One afternoon my sister, Anne, got on a bus on her way home to find the poet already sitting in a front seat, obviously deep in the throes of composition. So she left him alone and took a seat near the back. In due course they both got off the bus at the family gate and, as they went in, he looked at her vaguely and asked, 'Who is it you are looking for'?

Increasingly as he grew older and more feeble, the mental strain of composition grew greater. My mother therefore introduced him to detective stories, and often when exhausted by his struggle with a stubborn poem, he would read one of these for half an hour before returning to the struggle with renewed vigour. He continued to the very end to write poetry, and to carry on the endless task of revision. Even two days before he died he made some corrections to a poem and a play.

In his last years he seldom left the house, going out only when it seemed essential. It was arranged one day that a barber would come out from town to cut his hair, and they retreated to the bathroom at the top of the house. After a good deal of scrabbling round, my father called down the stairs to my mother, asking where they would find the electric wall-plug; so she had to remind him that there was no electricity in the house.

He continued always to make occasional visits to the Abbey Theatre, either to take part in Directors' meetings or else to attend performances of plays. I remember (as a teenager) one evening when I was alone with my father at the theatre. He was sitting in his favourite seat in the third row, and I was in the next seat, neither of us, as usual, saying anything. In the interval my father went out and a man next to me leaned over and said, 'Do you know who that is? That is W.B. Yeats.' I was too embarrassed to explain that I knew that, that he was in fact my father.

Throughout my childhood these visits to the Abbey Theatre were the only occasions when the whole family went out together. We went once a week, as a play seldom was kept longer than seven days. I remember well as a small child going home in a horse-cab from the Abbey after a performance, listening to my parents tearing the night's performance to shreds. The acting, the direction, the play itself, were all condemned. When I hear people talking about the 'great days' of the Abbey in times gone by, I tend to think about those rides in the horse-cab.

Unfortunately I was too young to be brought to the Abbey Theatre for the first performance in 1926 of Seán O'Casey's *Plough and the Stars*, which led to violent demonstrations by those who felt the play to be a slur on those who fought in 1916. However, my mother in later years told me something of what took place. It seems that a friend of the family who was sitting in the tenth row was so enraged at the demonstrators in the front seats that she took off one of her shoes to throw at them. But she threw it too hard and it landed on the stage, so she had the embarrassing task of hobbling round during the interval to recover it, and explaining how it happened that her shoe had landed on the stage amongst the actors.

A few years earlier, during the Civil War period in 1923, my mother was at the Abbey one night with Lady Gregory, who was staying with us at the time in Merrion Square. When they came out of the Theatre after the performance, gunfire could be heard, so my mother suggested that they take a horse-cab to get home. 'No we will not,' said Lady Gregory, 'I'm not going to give in to this.' And so they walked home. My English mother was indignant about this. 'It was all very well for her,' she said when she told the story, 'but it was nothing to do with me. Why should I get shot?'

On 13 June 1935, my father's seventieth birthday was celebrated. Messages of congratulation came from all over the world, and *The Irish Times* brought out a special supplement. He was delighted to be recognised in this way, and he must have looked back at those long years when he was faced with opposition on all sides in his efforts to bring about an Irish literary revival and to found a national theatre. By now he had succeeded in almost all his aims, and after these widespread birthday celebrations he must have been in no doubt that he was now accepted as Ireland's national poet.

Trinity College

I entered Trinity College in October, 1939, at a time when it had a small student body of around 1,200. There was no great problem in getting into College, all that was needed was a Pass in certain not too difficult examinations. There was no element of competition, no acquisition of 'points' was required. It was assumed as a matter of course in the 'Anglo-Irish' families of the day that in each generation the sons – and sometimes the daughters – would go to Trinity. Those who were not very bright could always get what was known as a 'Pass' degree, which gave them the right to put B.A. after their name without straining their intellect unduly in the process.

Trinity was the 'Protestant University', and each year in his Lenten Pastoral Archbishop John C. McQuaid would proclaim that there was a grave danger to the faith and morals of any Catholic going there. The Archbishop's worries about faith one could understand, but I doubt if he had any evidence that Trinity was a greater danger to student morals than was the largely Catholic National University. I can't say that in my student days I ever noticed any difference. At any rate the result of all this was that the student body in Trinity was overwhelmingly Protestant.

The administration of the College was in the hands of a group of mostly very old men whose offices were held for life, and whose thinking on Irish affairs had evolved way back in the nineteenth century. The student body, having grown up in the new Ireland, were somewhat less conservative in their political attitudes, but they were still strongly pro-British. In many respects the Trinity College of the 1940s was a backwater, hardly even a part of the nation. At that time its financial resources were so big that it could carry on without a State subsidy, and it was not until 1947 that for the first time a request was made for a £25,000 grant to renovate the College Green façade. They were given their money – the only query raised during Cabinet discussions was, why had it taken them so long to ask for a grant?

Even amongst the Trinity students of that day there was always the odd one who did not conform to the norm. At the time that I arrived on the scene there was, for example, a recent graduate who had the general reputation round College of being an eccentric left-wing radical. His name was Conor Cruise-O'Brien. I saw on a College notice-board a sheet of paper signed by him, asking anyone interested in reviving the defunct Dublin University Chess Club to come to a meeting at 11 a.m. on 11 November. Having always been a keen player, I decided to turn up.

Unfortunately he had forgotten that 11 November was Remembrance Day, when at 11 a.m. one was expected to stand, poppy-clad, for the two minute silence (at that period, the wearing of the poppy was looked upon as a Unionist manifestation). So when I wended my way across Front Square past the silent human statues, and arrived at the Chess Club rooms, he and I were the only ones there. We fixed a new date for the meeting, but in fact it was another 30 years before I saw him again. The result of this brief encounter was that I became Secretary of the Chess Club, a position I held for a number of years.

The great majority of my fellow-students, however, were very much under British influence, and in World War II, which had just begun, they of course supported the Allied cause. This was the only question on which I agreed with them, though for quite different reasons. They would have supported the 'British' side, no matter what the issues; I favoured the Allies for simple reasons of principle and international morality.

This was the period of the 'Emergency', when legislation enacted at the start of hostilities gave the Government power to control almost every aspect of the national life. Agriculture, industry, imports and exports, the rationing of scarce goods, fuel production, were all subject to control by Government Order. But the aspect of the 'Emergency' best remembered today is the censorship that – in effect – aimed to eliminate all adjectives from war reporting. In other words, activity on the various war fronts was to be reported deadpan; war communiques were to be printed or broadcast without comment. Not even the mildest criticism (or praise) of any of the combatants was allowed.

The theory underlying the censorship regime was that at all costs any public controversy must be avoided that might endanger our status of neutrality. There was a considerable element that would have liked to see us in the war on the allied side. On the other hand, there was a small pro-Nazi group in the country, and a much larger number that were anti-British on the age-old ground that Britain's weakness was Ireland's opportunity. In the absence of that censorship there would certainly have been a great deal of public discussion about the rights and wrongs of our neutrality. But I sometimes wondered what harm this would have done. Was it really true that one side or the other might attack us because of remarks made in the course of such internal debates?

At any rate, the censorship was rigid in the extreme, as might have been expected since it was under the overall control of Frank Aiken (the Minister for the Co-ordination of Defensive Measures). Aiken was of a dour and unyielding temperament, and from the first he showed a determination to achieve an absolute control over the media. With one exception, all newspapers were handed an elaborate list of things they were not allowed to say, and had to act as self-censors. *The Irish Times*, on the other hand, was not trusted to obey instructions, and an in-house censor was installed who read every word in the newspaper before publication was authorised. The result was a constant battle of wits between the newspaper and the censor. I remember a photograph appearing one day of a former *Irish Times* journalist, with a couple of paragraphs underneath saying that his numerous friends would be happy to hear that he had now recovered from his recent boating accident. Unknown to the censor, the 'recent boating accident' was the sinking by the Japanese of the British aircraft-carrier *Ark Royal*.

Nowadays those writing about the years of the 'Emergency' tend to make the assumption that during this period neutral Ireland was in a state of hibernation, knowing nothing of what was going on in the world. In fact newspaper readers were fed a constant diet of war news, and anyone who preferred their news to have a more lively and propagandist taste had only to listen to BBC Radio, which could be heard all over Ireland.

We ourselves had a radio set at home that had arrived in the late 1930s. My father had done some broadcasts for the BBC, and after one of these he was given (as part of his fee) the latest and most expensive model battery set available. We had never before had a set, and he rarely listened to it, just occasionally to the news. 'I beg your pardon,' he would say, if he had trouble hearing the announcer.

I used this set to get the latest war news from the BBC and also (on the short waves) from Germany, Italy and Soviet Russia. The propaganda put out by these three countries was mostly crude, though amusement could be had from the daily broadcasts from Germany by the Irishman William Joyce, who rapidly became known as Lord Haw Haw, because of the rich, plummy tones of his voice. He had a great sense of phrasing, and I well remember what was probably the last broadcast he made before his capture by the British forces at the end of the war in Europe. 'The Allies,' he proclaimed, 'may think that they have won the war, but they will soon find out that they cannot mop up the Bolshevik tide with democratic blotting paper.'

What may have seemed amusing to us in neutral Ireland, of course, was far from amusing to those in Britain who heard Lord Haw Haw jeering at them as the bombs rained down. One can perhaps understand why he was hanged for treason, even though he had never been a British citizen. But for a mere chance, however, he might never have lived to enjoy his wartime notoriety. Deputy Bobby Molloy told me once that in the year 1920 (during the War of Independence) his father was instructed to shoot the 20-year old Joyce as he came home for lunch in Galway City, where he then lived; it seems that he was informing on the IRA. Just that one day, however, Joyce did not come home, so he remained unshot.

It might have been thought that the official Government censorship was severe enough during the 'Emergency', but in Trinity College there was a further layer of censorship that had no connection with the reporting of war news. The various College Societies were forbidden to stage any political debates in public. Even the mildest topics of party politics had to be discussed in private, with a Chairman chosen from the College faculty. I used to go to meetings of the UCD Literary and Historical Society in

Earlsfort Terrace, and hear their fiery political debates, held in public with the press present. I envied them their democratic rights.

It is hard to see what purpose the Board of Trinity can have had in banning any public political debates, but it was presumably a result of their siege mentality at that time. They felt themselves surrounded by hostile elements who posed a constant threat to the independence of the College. Nothing must be said or done which could possibly cause offence to anyone outside the College walls. Even after the European war was over, they refused to make the College Dining Hall available for a speech by Harold Laski, a perfectly harmless English Marxist intellectual of the day (he wrote of the violent overthrow of the capitalist State, but would have been horrified had it happened).

If it was indeed the intention of the Board to avoid all controversy that might draw unfavourable attention on the College, then they ruined all their efforts through their inaction on VE Day (the day the war in Europe ended on 5 May 1945). I was in College, watching the 'celebrations' building up on that day. A large group of students began running round Front Square, brandishing a large Union Jack. These were mainly students from Northern Ireland, who had spent the War years in safety in Dublin – they had not even gone to study in Queen's University in Belfast, where the odd bomb might perhaps have fallen on them.

Then they went up to the roof of Regent House, overlooking College Green, where they hung up the Union Jack and the American flag; they then burned a Tricolour flag. This inflamed a counter-demonstration by students from UCD, including, it is said, a first public appearance by Charles J. Haughey. The Trinity porters (British ex-servicemen all), who could have removed those on the roof in five minutes if they had wanted to, were happy to leave them there, but locked all the College gates so that those violent Irish types outside could not get in. Though I did not know it at the time, my artist sister, Anne, was observing the scene in College Green and drawing pictures of the rioters in her sketch-book.

By chance I met in Front Square Dr Kenneth Claude Bailey, who held the position of Junior Dean and was therefore responsible for student discipline. He was a former British Army officer, and notoriously imperialist in his attitudes, so it was without much hope that I approached him and suggested that he should get the students down from the roof before something really serious happened. He did not even answer, but just turned away.

When I first went to Trinity I had no interest in debating, but after a few months I decided I should take part in the debates of the College Historical Society, as one means of lessening the shyness from which I had always suffered. In due course I became Auditor of the Society, and this involved the holding, in November 1944, of an Opening Meeting to inaugurate the new session. At this meeting I was expected to read a paper, and I decided that my subject would be 'The Small Nations'. I chose as my two main speakers Eamon de Valera and Jan Masaryk, Minister for Foreign Affairs in the Czechoslovak Government in exile in London (he was the son of the great T.G. Masaryk, the founder of the State of Czechoslovakia after the first World War).

In due course I turned up at Government Buildings, explained my business, and was brought in to see An Taoiseach. De Valera's first question was, who else had I invited to speak? As soon as I mentioned Jan Masaryk, he said 'Right, I will speak if he comes.' So I was left in the position that I would have both my main speakers, or neither of them. Time moved on, and even three weeks before the date of the meeting there was no reply from Masaryk. What I didn't realise was that he was perfectly willing to accept my invitation and de Valera was most anxious that he should come, but that there were prolonged negotiations as to the terms on which he could be allowed to come, without endangering our neutrality. It was agreed in the end that he would not speak at any political event in Ireland other than the College Historical Society, and so finally to my great relief I was told that he was coming.

In fact, even after all these negotiations there was still a diplomatic row over Jan Masaryk. A couple of days after my Opening Meeting he agreed to speak at a Society dealing with foreign affairs, thinking that it was a harmless non-political organisation. The Government, however, decided that this was a pressure group favouring Ireland's entry into the War on the Allied side, and the meeting was banned, causing much excitement in the newspapers. Two years later, Masaryk was dead: after the Communist takeover in Czechoslovakia, he fell to his death from a window in the Foreign Office in Prague. It has never been known for certain whether he was pushed or committed suicide in despair.

A few days before my Opening Meeting I was summoned to see the Provost, Dr Alton. He asked me to go to see de Valera, to invite him to come to dinner on Commons on the day of the meeting, to meet the Provost and Fellows of the College. So off I went again to Government Buildings and was brought in to see de Valera. He asked me to apologise to the Provost. 'You know,' he said, 'you may think it strange after all the years I have been in public life, but I still like to have some time to myself before making a speech.' However, he said, he would be happy to come to eat with the students after the meeting.

We students, of course, were delighted at this, but it was only years later that, thinking back, I realised how peculiar this whole affair was. Nowadays, should the Provost of Trinity College wish to send such an invitation to An Taoiseach he would presumably use the telephone, or write a note, or he might ask his secretary to deal with the matter. He would certainly not send round a student of the College to speak on his behalf. Dr Alton (at least to us students) seemed a shallow, rather foolish man, and I can only conclude that his strange behaviour reflected the nervousness felt by the College authorities at that period in their dealings with the 'new' Ireland outside the College Walls.

The year I spent as Auditor was not quite the end of my dealings with the College Historical Society; some years later I was drawn once again into its affairs on a question of women's rights. Women students in Trinity had traditionally suffered from various forms of discrimination. For example they were not allowed to stay in College after 6 p.m. Ultimately the women began to complain that it was unfair to them that they should have to leave the College Reading Room so early, while the male students could continue working there until it closed at 10 p.m. The authorities could not think of any legitimate answer to this, so they agreed to allow the women to work in the Reading Room until 10 p.m. But they were forbidden to go there on their own. After 6 p.m. they had to be escorted from the Front Gate by College porters, with a further escort out of College at 10 p.m. To let them loose on their own would clearly bring an end to civilization!

The College Historical Society had never had any but male members, so that women were totally excluded from the major debating society in College. Some 20 years after I had left Trinity there was a proposal to change the constitution so that women could be admitted to the Society, and a long series of 'Private Business' meetings was held to discuss the matter. As an ex-Auditor I was entitled to attend these meetings, so I duly turned up, to hear a series of fiery speeches defending the ancient traditions of the Society. Never since its foundation in 1770 had there been women members, so why now?

I was all for ancient tradition, but, after all, this one had started at a time when there were no women students in College, so it had little relevance to present-day conditions. I voted therefore in favour of admitting women, and the motion was passed by one vote. I have always maintained that it was my vote that did it, since if I had stayed at home that night the Society would have remained all-male.

As soon as the change was made, women students naturally began taking part in the activities of the Society, and in due course Mary Harney was elected as the first woman Auditor. Just four years later she was appointed by Jack Lynch to the Seanad, and she has now become the first woman to hold the position of Tánaiste.

There was one further event that took place while I was in Trinity, that brought about a fundamental change in my life. The Cumann Gaelach (Gaelic Society) at that time had as Auditor Peter Kavanagh, brother of the poet Patrick Kavanagh. Peter had none of his brother's genius, but a great many of his defects of character, so that he rapidly created chaos in the Cumann. I was present at one meeting where he ruled out of order any proposals of which he disapproved, so that in the end the assembled members lifted him bodily out of the Chair and forced him down the stairs.

Though the College authorities took a poor view of the affair, no one suffered any injury, and after more than 50 years it has become a long-forgotten student escapade. But for me there are excellent reasons for remembering that day's events in Trinity College: it was while Peter

Kavanagh was being pushed down the stairs that I first met Gráinne Ní Éigeartaigh whose elder brother, Seán, had organised the event. Gráinne and I had further meetings in quieter circumstances and a few years later, in 1949, we were married.

Apprentice Politician

During the years I spent in boarding schools, my developing interest in politics had of necessity been purely theoretical. Once I entered Trinity College in 1939, however, there was no longer anything to prevent my taking a more active part in political events. The only problem was that few political events were taking place. Because of the difficulties presented by the 'Emergency', political life was at a low ebb, and the Dáil elected in 1938 was allowed to continue for its full five years.

There was just one big public meeting during that period, an all-Party affair held in 1940 in College Green, to appeal for volunteers to join the Defence Forces. Eamon de Valera and William Cosgrave spoke, and I watched them with interest throughout the meeting. Though they sat close to each other in the front row on the platform, so far as I could see they did not exchange one word or greeting from start to finish. Co-operation in defence of our neutrality was one thing, reconciliation was quite another.

A couple of years later I joined the Local Defence Force (LDF) a part-time force intended to help out the Army in the event of an invasion. There was an LDF unit in Trinity, but I suspected that its defensive gaze was pointed in one direction only. I therefore headed for Portobello Barracks in Rathmines, and joined the 43rd Battalion – that would do its best, I thought, to resist invasion from whichever side it might come. Not that we would have been much use in beating off attacks from either a British or a German force.

Every Thursday evening we drilled assiduously on the barrack square, carrying ancient Lee-Enfield rifles, but we only fired these once a year when we were brought out to a firing range. I briefly acquired a reputation as a marksman, having achieved a bull's-eye at my first attempt; but I was never able to repeat this success. An Army Sergeant who was supervising operations finally diagnosed the problem: I was firing with my eyes shut.

The long-delayed General Election was held in 1943, and it was during the campaign that I joined Fianna Fáil. I had gone to a public meeting held by Seán MacEntee at one of the canal bridges, and before the meeting I went up to the platform and offered my services. I was given a few cards to hand out, and the following day I was sent to canvass the inhabitants of Dartry Road, in Rathmines. As an obvious innocent, I was not trusted with a copy of the electoral register (always scarce), but I was to go from door to door and hope for the best. The first place I went to was a large detached house lived in by just one severe old lady. She looked at me like something the cat had brought in, and sent me off in some disorder. On my way down the drive I noticed a tiny gate lodge, so I tried this, and found to my delight that it housed a half dozen fanatical Fianna Fáil voters. This taught me a valuable lesson about the democratic system.

After the election I was invited to join the Party, so I became a member of the Fintan Lalor Cumann in Rathmines. This was a big Cumann, with over a hundred members. I attended meetings assiduously, and in the 1944 General Election that followed shortly I began to learn something of the art of canvassing for votes. Four years later, in 1948, I was asked to run for the Dáil, and was selected by the convention to stand alongside Seán MacEntee in the three-seat constituency of Dublin South-East.

This was very much a baptism of fire. The Fianna Fáil Government's most dangerous antagonist in the 1948 General Election was the Clann na Poblachta party, which had been established by Seán MacBride as a new radical republican party. It was running a very active campaign, and there was a great deal of acrimony. I had never before stood on a platform, and I had to learn to deal with some very hostile crowds. Most of the hostility, of course, was directed at Seán MacEntee, who used all his considerable powers of invective against the Clann. When the votes were counted John A. Costello came first, followed by Seán MacEntee and Noel Browne; I came next with just under 3,000 first preference votes. On election day MacEntee and I did the usual tour of the polling stations, and we met Browne along the way. MacEntee in his usual affable way offered his hand to Browne, who refused to take it – an early warning, perhaps, of difficulties to come in later years.

As a result of the 1948 election Fianna Fáil lost office for the first time in 16 years, being replaced by a coalition Government led by John A. Costello, consisting of five parties and some independents. This curiously formed Government lasted for three years, until it broke up in 1951 as a result of an internal crisis. At the 1948 Fianna Fáil Árd Fheis I was elected a member of the National Executive (Committee of 15), and remained a member of that body for a number of years.

As might be expected, much time was spent by the Executive in the 1948–51 period on matters concerning the organisation, that had been badly hit by the rise of Clann na Poblachta. There were also the usual discussions on those perennial topics, Partition and the Irish language. The language problem was dealt with by the setting up of a committee, of which I became a member. I don't know whether this committee would ever have come up with any intelligent proposals, but in fact it was dominated by Frank Aiken, which ensured that nothing would be done. Aiken was an enthusiast for the revival of Irish, but had no new ideas at all as to how this might be achieved. At one meeting I ventured to make some suggestion – I don't remember what. It may well have been a foolish idea, but rather than deal with it on its merits (or lack of them), Aiken looked at me in a pained way and said 'tá tú óg'. Such an attitude might have been understandable coming from an old man, but Aiken at the time was just 52.

There was little discussion about new policies with which the next General Election might be contested. There was a general feeling that Fianna Fáil had lost office by a sort of accident, which would certainly be remedied the next time. The public would see the light, and would return the Party to its natural place in government.

As a result, when the coalition Government fell in 1951, Fianna Fáil faced the election with nothing new to offer. Nothing had been learned from the defeat of 1948, a defeat due in part at least to a general feeling that Fianna Fáil Ministers had grown tired after 16 consecutive years in office. In spite of the inglorious collapse of the Costello Government, Fianna Fáil gained only one seat, and in order to get into office had to rely on the support of five Independents. I was again a candidate in this election, in competition once more with Seán MacEntee, John A. Costello (the outgoing Taoiseach), and Noel Browne. Each of these was well over the quota on the first count, I scraped up a couple of thousand votes, and the rest of the field got in the hundreds. After the election, to my great surprise I was nominated to the Seanad by Eamon de Valera, who once again was Taoiseach. So overnight I found myself directly involved in public life; it was the beginning of a career in politics that lasted until I retired some 30 years later.

I had to settle in at once to learn about the sometimes arcane procedures of the Seanad, and to get to know my fellow-members, none of whom I had ever met. The first of these that I did come across was Senator Margaret Pearse (sister of Patrick Pearse) who came over to speak to me in the Dáil restaurant. This was the first time I had been in the restaurant and, seeing that one side of the room was much less crowded than the other, I had sat down there. Senator Pearse thereupon appeared and asked me why I was sitting there. 'Why not?' I asked, so she explained that I was sitting on the Fine Gael side of the room, instead of on my own Fianna Fáil side. The theory was, I gathered, that one's conversation should not be heard by 'enemy' ears. This was the only time I ever spoke to Margaret Pearse, and it was the only political contribution I ever heard her make.

At that time – the early 1950s – there were still some members of the Parliamentary Party who had been active in the 1916–23 years. Dan Breen was one of them, a revered figure who was re-elected at every election by his Tipperary constituents. It was alleged that the bullets still lodged in various parts of his body tended to cause him pain at the start of an election campaign, so that he could campaign from his bed and thereby gain a big sympathy vote. I only remember one speech that he made at a meeting of the Parliamentary Party. We were discussing (in 1953) some health legislation that was being opposed by the Catholic hierarchy, when Dan Breen stood up and said 'It's a terrible pity that 30 years ago, when we had the chance, we didn't shoot a few Bishops.' No one else made any comment on this, though Eamon de Valera looked glum.

Another veteran was Mark Killilea (father of the present-day MEP), who told me once of his activities in Co. Wexford during the 1918 General Election. This was the election that paved the way for Irish Independence with the return of an overwhelming majority of republican candidates. It seems that Mark had acquired one of the few motor cars in the County, and so on polling day he was able to vote for Sinn Féin 167 times! He had another anecdote about the Civil War period, when he was one of several hundred Republicans held in a Dublin prison. In each cell there was a large copy of the Holy Bible with a cover about an inch thick. At a certain time each day the cell doors were opened for a brief period, and it was agreed that on a given signal the Bible in each cell would be placed just behind the door's hinges. A couple of strong men pulling on the cell door easily broke the hinges, and the doors were then thrown over the balcony railing into the well below. There was no effort by the prisoners to escape, but the prison was made unusable until repairs had been done.

One of the most popular members of the Party was Bob Briscoe, who in later years gained instant celebrity in the United States on his becoming Lord Mayor of Dublin. To Americans it was inconceivable that a Jew could become Lord Mayor of 'Catholic Dublin'; they could not understand that in Ireland, belonging to a minority religion was no hindrance to a person's success in public life. In the Parliamentary Party, while we of course knew that Bob Briscoe was a Jew, this was not a matter that normally concerned us. There was perhaps one exception to this, Senator Andy Clarkin, who was a particularly pious Catholic. Bob told me once that he and the Senator were in a long line at a Presidential reception waiting to meet Cardinal Cushing of Boston, who was on an official visit. Andy Clarkin impressed on Bob that at all costs he must kneel and kiss the Cardinal's ring, and as they waited he kept on repeating this advice at five-minute intervals. Finally they reached the top of the line, and Bob Briscoe held out his hand, saying that he was afraid that as a Jew he could not kiss the Cardinal's ring. Cardinal Cushing shook his hand with enthusiasm, telling him 'My sister married one of you fellas.'

In the years immediately after the War, Bob Briscoe was active in support of the struggle to set up an independent State of Israel. He collected money for the resistance organisation Irgun Zwai Leumi, a fact well known to de Valera, who favoured the cause of Jewish independence, and so chose to ignore Bob's activities.

One of Bob's best-known characteristics was his optimism, which he carried sometimes to absurd lengths. At election time, no matter how gloomy the omens were, he was invariably convinced that Fianna Fáil would win. This became known to the betting men on the Opposition side, who used their knowledge to win large sums from him. At the opposite extreme was Eamon de Valera's son Vivion, who could never even envisage the possibility that an election might be won.

The Minister for Posts and Telegraphs at that time was Erskine Childers, whom I got to know fairly well. He was able and intelligent, with imagination and a wide range of ideas, but somehow he never made the political progress that one might have expected. In later years he went on to deal with Lands and Fisheries, Health, and a new Transport and Power Ministry set up by Seán Lemass. None of these could be described as a senior Ministry.

I think one of his problems was that his ideas were not always practical, and he tended to hand out advice to all and sundry; unsolicited advice is by no means always welcome. Certainly his colleagues in Government sometimes took a slightly cynical view of his capabilities. At the time of the 1957 election I was trying to put together a Fianna Fáil policy document, based on the reports of various party committees that had been meeting for the past couple of years. The committee dealing with farming policy had never finished its work, so I had to assemble something from the bits and pieces of paper that had been left behind when the Deputies went off to the hustings. When I had the job done I went to Seán Lemass with it, and said that the ground seemed to be pretty well covered, but that we had nothing on poultry. 'Give it to Childers', said Lemass instantly, 'he'd write about anything'. So I rang up Childers, and sure enough, next day, there appeared six pages of a policy on poultry. I cut this to six lines, which was about what the topic seemed to be worth, and everyone was happy.

Childers was a vociferous supporter of all things cultural, given to the public recitation of poetry. He came up to me once and said 'Do you know what I did last night? I realised that it was a long time since I read your father's poems, so I went to bed with the Collected Poems' (this is a book of 550 pages). 'And,' he said, 'I didn't put the light out until I finished it.' It seemed a strange way to read poetry.

Erskine Childers represented first Longford-Westmeath and then Monaghan, but he would have been much better suited to one of the middle-class areas of South Dublin. He told me once of his embarrassment when one morning in his Ministerial office he had a telephone call from one of his constituents, to say that her unmarried and pregnant daughter was at that moment on a train from Longford. Would the Minister meet her at one of the Dublin stations and bring her to Holles Street hospital? So he duly set off in his State car and did as he was asked.

Nowadays Childers is often condemned for his action in closing down the suburban railway line from Harcourt Street to Bray. My personal view – a minority one – is that he was perfectly right, since hardly anyone used it: there was little interest in a train that ended at Harcourt Street, a place to which no one wanted to go. It is now proposed to run the LUAS light-rail service along the old Harcourt Street line, but this will go right into the City centre, which will make all the difference. A much more substantial service that Childers closed was the old West Cork line, resulting in bitter complaints. A high-powered delegation of Cork business-men came up to protest to the Minister, who later told me what happened. When the two dozen or so indignant Corkmen were assembled in his office, he asked anyone to put up a hand who had come to Dublin that day by train. Not one hand appeared, so Childers suggested that no more need be said. They themselves had shown the problem he faced in trying to save the rail passenger services; and he ushered the delegation out.

Some twenty years after I first met Erskine Childers, he was one of those being suggested as a possible Presidential candidate to succeed de Valera. I found that Deputies with whom I discussed the question were very much opposed to the idea: he was, they said, extremely unpopular in the Party. I was surprised, as I always found him pleasant to deal with.

I asked what was the problem. I was told that he would walk straight past a colleague of long standing without the slightest greeting. When I suggested that perhaps he was shy, or just did not notice people (I was thinking of my father), they said that wasn't it at all – he simply felt superior to others. At the General Election in 1969, it was claimed, when his constituency colleague Paddy Mooney lost his seat in Monaghan, Erskine walked out of the count and went back to Dublin in his state car, without saying one single word to the unfortunate loser. Whatever about all this, Childers did in the end become an extremely popular President; but sadly he died suddenly after only a year in office.

Apart from the many back-bench members of the Party who had been in Fianna Fáil since the very early days, there were also a number of Ministers who had first come to office in 1932. When de Valera returned to power in 1951, he made only two changes in his Cabinet – thus hardly suggesting that any new or progressive policies could be expected. The most significant of his appointments was that of Seán MacEntee to be Minister for Finance.

MacEntee was one of the ablest of the Fianna Fáil Ministers, and over the years he had been one of de Valera's closest and most influential advisers. Unpopular with the public because of his aggressive platform style, he could be pleasant and amiable in private. In his youth he had written some poetry, and it was perhaps his memory of this that on one occasion saved the writer Myles na gCopaleen from disaster. Myles (in private life known as Brian O'Nolan) was a civil servant in the Department of Local Government. Unfortunately he was an alcoholic, and one day the Secretary of the Department came to the Minister (Seán MacEntee) with a long list of O'Nolan's deficiencies as an official. The time had come, it was suggested, when he really must be let go. 'No,' MacEntee said, 'the Department of Local Government can afford to maintain one mad genius.' But some years later there were Ministerial changes, and that unimaginative Cavan man Paddy Smith took over the Department. This time there was no reprieve for Myles na gCopaleen.

In appointing Seán MacEntee to Finance, de Valera ensured that no progressive or expansionary policies would be carried out in the lifetime of that Government. MacEntee was extremely conservative in economic matters, and his thinking was in perfect conformity with the prevailing attitudes held in the Department. The result was the notorious Budget of 1952: income tax went up by 5 per cent, and there were rises in the price of tea, bread, butter, milk, sugar and alcohol. Nothing like this had been expected – indeed never before had there been a Budget as severe as this. From an economist's point of view the Budget was a success – not for nothing has economics been described as 'the dismal science'. A year later the balance of payments had improved, and imports and domestic consumption were down. In other words, at a time of much poverty, high emigration and unemployment, the effect of Seán MacEntee's Budget had been to reduce still further the public's limited spending power. Ireland had come through the years of the 'Emergency', when economic activity had practically shut down, and little had been done since then to overcome the resulting depression. The 1950s were a time of general gloom; emigration was so high that books were being published under titles such as *The Vanishing Irish*.

What was needed at this time was a Budget that would offer at least some hope of a more prosperous future. What was handed out was a programme of yet more gloom and austerity. Austerity had been accepted in defence of our neutrality, but it was less acceptable in defence of the balance of payments. Obviously the balance of payments problem needed to be dealt with, but many of us in the Parliamentary Party felt that MacEntee had gone much too far in accepting the medicine handed out by the excessively conservative Department of Finance.

After some time it became clear that many Fianna Fáil Deputies and Senators were very unhappy with the economic policy being carried out by the Government. So I decided to raise the matter at a Party meeting. To do this I needed an ally amongst the Deputies, and recruited Frank Carter, of Longford: he had been amongst the strongest critics in private of the Budget. I drafted a motion criticising the policies of Seán MacEntee, and between us we collected 35 signatures to it and gave it in to the Party chairman. The result was an animated debate that stretched over two days. Inevitably our motion was defeated, though as I walked out of the room at the end, Seán Lemass said in my ear, 'Never mind Senator, you were 98 per cent right.'

The Fianna Fáil Government's Dáil position had been weak from the start, and after three years a new election could no longer be avoided. Fianna Fáil lost four seats, and were ten seats short of an overall majority. In May, 1954, a new Coalition was formed, again under John A. Costello as Taoiseach. I therefore lost my Seanad seat, and did not regain it until the Seanad election in 1961. In the meantime, however, I continued to attend meetings of the National Executive in my capacity as Publicity Officer.

Noel Browne

It is now 50 years since Noel Browne became Minister for Health in the Coalition Government of John A. Costello. He brought down that Government. He belonged to several political parties and fought with them all. He quarrelled with almost all his friends and collaborators. Over the years he grew steadily more embittered, more convinced that at all times in his political career he, and only he, was in the right. And yet the universal tributes paid to him at his death in May 1997, showed that for the people of Ireland, a majority of whom were not even born when he first came into politics, Noel Browne remained one of the great heroes of modern Irish history.

Even for those too young to have had first-hand experience of the scourge of tuberculosis, there is a sort of folk memory of its effects on thousands of families all over Ireland. It was a disease that bred on poverty, on over-crowded housing conditions. Until the advent of the new drugs, there was no real cure for TB. In places such as Davos, in Switzerland, whole hillsides were covered in gleaming white sanatoria, where the rich came from all over Europe to be treated by the finest doctors in comfortable surroundings. But they died all the same.

In Ireland there was no Davos, and once one member of a family got the disease, there was a good chance that it would spread throughout the household: more than 4,000 died each year. When Noel Browne became Minister for Health in 1948, he decided to deal with TB as a national emergency and he provided in two years some 2,000 beds for TB patients. With the aid of the new miracle drugs, the curse of tuberculosis was effectively ended.

Dr Browne was a member of an extremely conservative Government, but he was fortunate in being able to carry out his hospital programme without having to go through any of the normal Cabinet procedures. He had complete control over the Hospital Sweeps funds, and could use them as he wished without reference to anyone. These funds had been built up over many years from the sale of Sweep tickets, and previous Ministers for Health had used only the funds' investment income for hospital building. Now Dr Browne took over the entire capital fund to finance his campaign against TB.

But things were different when he embarked on a new Mother and Child Scheme, aiming to provide (without any means test) free medical and hospital care for mothers and their children up to the age of 16. He did not understand that all the details had to be approved in advance by his fellow Ministers. They, along with the doctors' organisations, opposed his ideas as 'socialised medicine', and once objections began coming from the Catholic hierarchy, his colleagues in Government seized on this as an excuse for condemning his proposals. There was a bizarre period during which day after day brightly coloured brochures were being sent out from the Department of Health publicising a Mother and Child Scheme, the details of which had never been approved by the Cabinet. There could only be one end to all this. Dr Browne's position was already very weak; it became impossible when his own Clann na Poblachta party leader turned against him. Once the Bishops had spoken, Seán MacBride said, then the Mother and Child Scheme must be abandoned. Noel Browne resigned as Minister for Health on the instructions of Seán MacBride, and was expelled from Clann na Poblachta. Shortly after this, the Government fell, and a General Election had to be held, in May 1951.

When, after the election, Eamon de Valera was put forward again as Taoiseach, he had the support of Noel Browne, who for the next couple of years retained his status as an Independent, while continuing to support the Fianna Fáil Government. In his autobiography *Against the Tide* (published in 1986), he explained that he was able to support MacEntee's economic policies because, he said, he chose to ignore those policies disagreeable to him in order to concentrate on the issue of the health services.

The health services to which he referred were the provisions of the Mother and Child Scheme that had collapsed under the previous Coalition. Dr James Ryan, the new Minister for Health, had the task of getting as much as possible of this Scheme through the Oireachtas. In his Autobiography, Noel Browne dealt at considerable length with the negotiations that took place between the Government and the Bishops. He claimed that at every single point Fianna Fáil gave way: 'All pretence at being independent members of the Cabinet of a sovereign Parliament had been abandoned.'

In fact, Dr Browne, writing over 30 years later, apparently suffered from a lapse of memory. When the Bill incorporating the new Mother and Child Scheme was introduced by Dr Ryan, Noel Browne had no apparent difficulty in voting for it at every stage. Not only that, but just one month after the legislation finally became law, he applied (in November 1953) to join Fianna Fáil. That was not the action of a man who was dissatisfied with an item of legislation that he had declared to be the only thing in the entire Dáil session that was of any interest to him.

Noel Browne's arrival was welcomed at every level in Fianna Fáil. There were just a few conservatives of the MacEntee stamp who had reservations, but they were very much in the minority. After his arrival Noel, also, was clearly pleased he was amongst us. As we were leaving at the end of the first Parliamentary Party meeting that he attended – it had gone on all day – I apologised for its interminable length. 'Not at all,' he said, 'I was delighted to be able to listen to all these criticisms of Government policy. You know, I am used to a party (Clann na Poblachta) in which, should there be the slightest criticism, then someone proposes a vote of confidence in the leader.' I had in fact heard (in earlier years) about Noel's various disputes with his former Party leader, Seán MacBride. It was alleged that MacBride kept detailed files on all the members of the Clann na Poblachta Executive. At one Clann meeting he had attacked Dr Browne for allowing himself to be photographed by *The Irish Times* shaking hands with the Church of Ireland Archbishop of Dublin.

In the General Election of June 1954, there was only one seat for Fianna Fáil in Dublin South-East, and this was won by MacEntee, with about 300 votes on the last count between him and Noel Browne. Browne could certainly have won a Seanad seat, but chose not to stand. He did however remain very active in the Fianna Fáil organisation. At the Árd Fheis he was elected to the position of Hon. Treasurer, a very unusual honour for such a new recruit. This was a clear demonstration of the respect in which he was held by the thousands of Fianna Fáil supporters who came from all over the country to take part in the Árd-Fheis.

At the National Executive Noel Browne produced a Memorandum on the subject of the educational system, and after some discussion it was decided to set up a Committee to make proposals for reform. Noel of course was made a member, as well as Eoin Ryan, Brian Lenihan, Seán Moylan, Michael ffrench O'Carroll and others. I was appointed Secretary. This Committee met on numerous occasions over a period of six months, and from the first I was puzzled at how little Noel had to contribute. He certainly had numerous criticisms to make, but did not seem to be able to translate these into practical proposals. Outside his own field of expertise – the health services – he seemed quite ill-informed.

The other members of the Committee all had suggestions to offer, as I did myself, and it fell to me as Secretary to do the basic research on which the Report was based, and to draft all the numerous proposals it contained. The Committee members were mostly of the younger generation, and so we were not limited in our thinking by traditional attitudes.

The discussions at the National Executive on our Report took place at ten successive meetings, and as the person who had done all the drafting it fell to me in particular to defend the Report line by line. In the end we got very nearly all our proposals through. As regards National schools, it was agreed to raise the schools' building rate by 50 per cent, and that the maintenance of school buildings would now be the responsibility of the State. Various steps were approved for increasing the number of teachers, in order to reduce the excessive size of classes. The period of compulsory education was to be extended from the age of 14 to 15. A number of steps were agreed for the development of full-time vocational education; additional expenditure involved was to be paid by the State, as was the cost of the increases proposed in Secondary and University scholarships. Amongst other proposals agreed was one providing that a much increased stress should be laid on oral Irish at all school levels. We also proposed the removal of the Marriage Ban, under which women teachers in National schools had to give up their posts when they got married. No decision on this question was taken at the National Executive, but on the return to office of Fianna Fáil in 1957, the Marriage Ban on women teachers was abolished.

In his Autobiography, Noel Browne wrote that he was happy with the Report, and with its reception by the National Executive. But he went on to say that, after the Report had been accepted, de Valera said that of course it must be understood 'that the recommendations will be implemented when financial considerations permit.' I have no memory of his saying this, though there is no reason why I should remember. For most people, it would seem merely a statement of the obvious. But for Browne – 30 years later – 'with that handful of words, our valuable and useful work had come to naught.' He said nothing to me, but continued to convey the impression that he was very happy at the outcome of his Memorandum on education.

All this suggests that Noel Browne never understood (to use the old cliché) that politics is the art of the possible. It is simply not realistic for anyone in Government to say, 'We will carry out this policy whether we have the money or not.' For me, the important thing was that at the next (1956) Árd Fheis, Seán Lemass arranged for me to explain in detail the proposals set out in our Report and accepted by the National Executive. Thus in the most formal and public manner they were announced as official Party policy.

In 1957 the second Coalition Government fell, when Seán MacBride withdrew his support, and all Parties began preparing for the General Election that followed. In my own constituency of Dublin South-East, preparations were under way for the convention to select Dáil candidates, and the word went round that Seán MacEntee and his constituency supporters were planning to deprive Noel Browne of the nomination. The excuse given was that he had been making Socialist speeches that bore no relation to the policies of Fianna Fáil. This indeed was true, but it was up to de Valera to warn him that he was in risk of endangering his membership of the Party. In the absence of such a warning, Dr Browne was entitled to assume that he had committed no offence.

In any event the campaign against Noel Browne had quite a different cause. In the 1954 election, he had almost defeated Seán MacEntee, and the MacEntee faction in the constituency was determined not to run such a risk again. Just a few days before the date of the selection Convention there occurred an incident that I have never been able to forget. Noel Browne and I were sitting together after a meeting of the Dublin South-East Comhairle Ceantair (Constituency Council), when Seán MacEntee came over and greeted Noel affably; he continued for some time to carry on a most friendly conversation. Everyone in the room knew what was going on, that MacEntee was engaged in a plot to destroy Dr Browne's political career. Only poor Noel, a political innocent abroad, knew nothing of all this. So far as he was concerned he assumed he was going to be chosen as the Fianna Fáil candidate to stand with Seán MacEntee.

In the next few days I contacted Convention delegates, pointing out that he was accepted by the National Executive as a member in good standing of Fianna Fáil, and that it was the duty of the Convention to pick the candidate with the strongest electoral base. I was wasting my time, and the only effect was to label me in certain quarters as a sort of enemy in the ranks. At the Convention Noel Browne was replaced as a candidate by Seán Moore, who in this election had absolutely no chance of being elected (though he did gain election in later years).

There was one further stage to be gone through in this affair. At every election the National Executive has to consider the result of each Convention throughout the country, and can add a name if it is felt that the panel of candidates is not strong enough. In due time they came to Dublin South-East, and there was a long debate as to whether Dr Noel Browne should be added to the list. It became clear that there would be a majority in favour of adding his name.

At this stage Seán MacEntee rose to speak. His message was simple: he himself was not prepared to stand for election alongside Noel Browne. That was the end. On the eve of an election it was simply not conceivable that one of the most senior people in the Party should be lost under such circumstances. There was great resentment at MacEntee's attitude, much sympathy for Dr Browne, and a general feeling that we had probably lost a second Fianna Fáil seat in the constituency. I was sent down to talk to Noel, who had been waiting below during the National Executive debate. He was of course deeply upset. He stood as an Independent candidate in the election and was easily elected. Under Party rules he was then automatically expelled.

I have sometimes wondered what would have happened had Noel Browne gained a Fianna Fáil nomination in 1957. No matter what he may have written since, he was, I think, happy with his membership – after all, he did seek a Party nomination at the election. While he considered de Valera to be excessively conservative, he admired Lemass, and would presumably have welcomed his becoming Taoiseach in 1959. But in the long run, I doubt if he would have stayed in the Party. Not for him were the compromises inherent in membership of any political party, and sooner or later he would have left. His subsequent career showed beyond doubt that, as he grew older, for Noel Browne the only political views worth considering were his own.

Eamon de Valera

At the time I became active in politics, Eamon de Valera was still the dominant figure in Irish public life. He was the 'last Commandant' of 1916, the founder of Fianna Fáil in 1926. In the 1930s he had got rid of the Oath of Allegiance and all the other restrictions on sovereignty contained in the Treaty document. He had created the 1937 Constitution. In 1938 he had made our later neutrality possible by getting back the four 'Treaty ports' and at the same time ending the 'Treaty clauses' which gave Britain in time of war the right to use Irish soil as a war base. Finally, at the time I joined Fianna Fáil, he was steering neutral Ireland successfully through the World War period.

Eamon de Valera, today, gets a bad press. The cult of revisionism is in full swing, and it sometimes seems, almost, as if an attempt is being made to write him out of Irish history. Some of our revisionist writers give the impression that all they know about this towering figure in modern Irish history is his St Patrick's Day speech on 'The Ireland we have Dreamed of', with its reference to 'the contests of athletic youths and the laughter of happy maidens, whose fire-sides would be forums for serene old age' (the maidens were in fact 'happy', not 'comely', as is always stated today). I listened to that 1943 broadcast, which I do not remember causing any particular comment. As a serious declaration of policy it would have been ridiculous, but it was accepted that he was merely looking back in a reminiscent way to an ideal rural Ireland that, if it ever existed, had long since disappeared. But now, after 50 years, it seems that no discussion of de Valera's long career can take place without some reference to these long-forgotten 'happy maidens'.

Why their sudden reappearance? It seems that these maidens fit in conveniently with the revisionist concept of de Valera as an austere individual who presided over an Ireland that was narrow, conservative and backward looking in its thinking. It was only with his departure from the political scene, we are told, that a new and liberal Ireland could arise. This interpretation of modern Irish history ignores the fact that for nearly half the time that de Valera was active in politics he was not even in office. It was others who brought in the censorship of books, it was others who first brought in the ban on divorce. It was others who abandoned Dr Browne's Mother and Child Scheme because they were not willing to risk a 'belt from a crozier'. De Valera was certainly very conservative in his thinking, but in this he was typical of the Irish people and politicians of his day.

There has indeed been a revolution in public attitudes in the past 35 years. There were many reasons for this, Vatican II, the coming of Television, improvements in education, the replacement of a rural by an urban society. The retirement of de Valera had nothing to do with it: if the political leaders of today have changed, it is because society itself has changed.

However, his retirement was of course an important political event, not least because it was so long awaited. For Eamon de Valera, the safeguarding of Irish neutrality during the World War, ending with his brilliant reply to Churchill's arrogant victory speech in which he attacked Irish neutrality, was the culmination of his long career. After that there was little left for him to achieve. What post-War Ireland needed was a whole range of new social and economic policies that could transform living standards and give the Irish people some hope for a better future. In principle, de Valera was in favour of all this, but he would not accept that as a first step he must bring new blood into the Government, to replace those who had grown old and tired in office.

When he returned to office in 1951 he kept on almost all his Ministers from earlier years, with the conservative Seán MacEntee in a pivotal position as Minister for Finance. De Valera himself was now in his seventies. It is not surprising that there were no new initiatives of importance during the life of that Government. On economic questions he became ever more conservative as he grew older, and he was given to the making of long speeches on obscure economic topics.

I remember one night in Bray town, during a Wicklow by-election, when he lectured us all, for a full hour, with the rain pelting down, on the topic of external assets. There were numerous matters that might have been of interest to the voters of Bray, but the question of our external assets was not one of them. I have often wondered whether de Valera was an eloquent platform orator in his younger days, for by the time I first heard him, his speeches were generally not calculated to hold an audience. We would cheer him to the echo as he rose to speak, but the speech itself was almost invariably a disappointment.

Though I had some brief dealings with de Valera in 1944, it was only when I became a member of the Fianna Fáil National Executive after 1948 that I was able to observe him in action. It was interesting to watch him presiding at meetings. He was no dictator, would never instruct the members as to what decision they should take on any particular issue; but he hardly ever failed to get the decision he wanted from them. He would allow the debate on a contentious matter to drag on until everyone was exhausted, expressing no opinion himself. Then he would summarise at some length what had been said, finishing by saying that in the light of all these arguments he felt that such-and-such a decision would be best. And we would agree.

But even de Valera, with all his authority, did not always get his way. He would go down to some rural constituency to preside at an election Convention, and would open the proceedings by addressing the delegates. On occasion he would give some advice as to the type of candidate who should be selected – someone, perhaps, who was young, with various excellent qualifications that he would list and, of course, a fine command of the Irish language. This description would match exactly one of the hopeful candidates, who would immediately lose whatever support he had previously garnered. The Convention delegates would have died for de Valera, but they were not going to allow any interference with their right to choose candidates.

In the achievement of his national aims, Eamon de Valera had been almost entirely successful. Yet he failed in his efforts to revive the Irish language, the matter perhaps dearest to his heart. In every public speech he would stress the importance of the language, and call upon the people to learn to speak it. Many did, of course, but for the majority it was too burdensome a task. He never was prepared to accept that the schools were failing to produce speakers of Irish, and that some new system would have to be devised. The Constitution of Fianna Fáil included as one of the Party's aims 'the restoration of the Irish language as the spoken language of the people...' One wonders why he did not insist that the schools should have regard to this aim, rather than concentrating on the reading and writing of the language?

At the National Executive there were numerous debates on the language. After a few of these had taken place, I came to realise that de Valera was unwilling to agree to any proposals that would require more than a minimum of State funding. The implications of such an attitude became clear to me when my wife, Gráinne, and I began looking for books for our children who were being brought up as Irish speakers. An Gúm, the Government company that was supposed to be producing books in Irish, was (at that period) notoriously inefficient, but I went in one day to their office and bought a copy of their Catalogue. 'A lot of these books are out of print', said the amiable man behind the counter. 'Well,' I asked, 'do you have a list of the out of print books?' 'We do indeed,' he said, 'but it's out of print'. It had in fact, become only too clear that An Gúm was not going to provide the books that were so essential to the language movement. My brother-in-law Seán Ó hÉigeartaigh therefore set up his own publishing firm, Sáirséal agus Dill, and for the first time a whole range of attractively produced books became available.

Eamon de Valera was immensely enthusiastic for the language, and he had the authority to insist that everything necessary was done to secure the campaign's success. But he never seemed to be able to decide just what was needed to save the language – or even to accept that something more was needed than was already being done. Some useful steps were taken with his encouragement, but they were never enough, and the Irish language continued to decline.

De Valera's second great failure was in relation to the Partition of Ireland: he did not understand, or else ignored, the real problem that had to be faced in any effort to reunite the country. He rightly stressed the injustice of the division of Ireland and the discrimination exercised against the minority in the North. However, he rarely made any reference to the existence of a Protestant majority in the North who did not want to come in to a united Ireland. For example, in a 1938 message to an anti-Partition rally in Derry, de Valera said:

> *I regard the ending of the unnatural division of our country as a matter of vital concern, not merely for the people of the Six Counties who are suffering from it, but for the people of all Ireland and for the Irish race throughout the world. It is also a matter of concern for the people of Britain.*

Although that message was sent some 20 years before de Valera's retirement from active politics, his thinking on the Partition problem never changed. We have the reference to the Nationalist minority who are suffering from Partition, and that it is of vital concern also 'for the people of all Ireland and for the Irish race throughout the world.' Presumably the million or so Unionists are concealed somewhere amongst 'the people of all Ireland'.

The frequent discussions on Partition at the National Executive, with Eamon de Valera presiding, naturally took a similar line. The Unionists, where they were mentioned, were looked on as people who had been misled, no doubt temporarily. Once they realised how well we treated our local minority, then they would gladly come in with us. There was much talk of Douglas Hyde and Erskine Childers. Occasionally Seán Lemass would speak, and I would go home convinced that he was the only person there who understood anything about Partition.

It is significant that within a few months of his becoming Taoiseach, in 1959, Seán Lemass made a major speech to the Oxford Union Society. He stressed the unfairness of the way Partition had been set up, the constant discrimination against the minority, and pointed out that no normal political development was possible in the Six County area. He stressed the simple truth that 'Ireland is one nation, in its history, in its geography and in its people, entitled to have its essential unity expressed in its political institutions.'

Where he diverged from the norm, however, was in his attitude to the Unionists of Northern Ireland. He accepted that they might fear that they would suffer disadvantage in a united Ireland because of their religion.

> *Our goal is the reunification of Ireland by agreement, and we cannot expect very speedy results. The barriers of fear and suspicion in the minds of the Unionists are too strong to be demolished quickly. For that reason our aim is to develop contacts which will tend to build goodwill and to strive for concerted action in particular fields where early practical advantages can be obtained, hoping to proceed step by step to a new situation in which a reappraisal of the whole problem can be undertaken, unhampered by prejudice.*

Seán Lemass in this speech set out a whole new approach to the Partition problem. Under the title 'One Nation' it was issued by Fianna Fáil as a pamphlet, which all units of the organisation were instructed to study. As it was so soon after the departure of the founder of the Party, nothing was said about a change of policy; the pamphlet purported to be merely a restatement of existing policies. But in fact it was clear that a new era had dawned, in this as in many other aspects of the national life.

It had been a long wait however. Eamon de Valera was in his seventies, almost blind, and with any other leader it would have been put to him that it was time for him to go. But he made it clear that he would stay 'as long as the organisation wants me.' No one in the organisation was prepared to raise that issue. He was the founder of Fianna Fáil, the only leader the party had ever had. There were discreet discussions about the matter – so discreet that no one is quite sure, even today, by what means it was suggested to him that he should become President of Ireland on Seán T. Ó Ceallaigh's departure from office in 1959. However it was done, he accepted that the time had come for him to retire from active politics, and he was duly nominated.

However, I suspect that he did not really welcome his retirement from active politics. He insisted on staying on as Taoiseach until the result of the

Presidential election had been declared. The only implication one can draw from this is, that in the (admittedly unlikely) event of his failing to be elected he would have wished to continue on as Taoiseach.

I was put in charge of the writing and publication of his Election Address. This was a massive affair, spread over four broadsheet newspaper pages, and included a detailed account of his entire life. It was only then that I realised just how difficult it was to reach final agreement with him on any draft. Time and time again I would think that everything was arranged, only to find that some matter of detail had to be changed. It was one of the happier moments of my life when I was finally able to give him my regrets, but that no further change could be made, as the Election Address was actually being printed.

A few years later I discussed these drafting problems with de Valera's faithful Secretary, Máire Ní Cheallaigh. She told me that, one night while he was President, they were working together on some document up to midnight, when she went home. At about 2 a.m. she was telephoned by the President, who had a further change that must be made. In the document they had inserted a number, 'twenty six', but this was an error: there should have been a hyphen between the 'twenty' and the 'six'.

Apart from his more formal activities as President, de Valera would occasionally invite little informal groups of friends or former party workers to spend an evening with him. It was on these occasions that he showed he was by no means as grim or austere as his public image might suggest. On one such evening he told us a story of his childhood. His uncle, with whom he lived on a five-acre farm in Bruree in West Limerick, used to send him out with the cattle (when he was around five years old) to feed on the 'long acre', the strip of grass along each side of the road. This was a useful source of pasture for those with very small farms. Grazing the 'long acre' was illegal, so he was told whenever a policeman hove in sight, to whip up the herd and pretend he was going somewhere with them. Listening to that story, I thought, who could have dreamt that the little boy would end up as President of Ireland.

He told us also, on one such occasion, of the period he spent teaching in Rockwell College. According to him, the teachers at the College were given to betting on horse races. On race days, of course, someone had to lay the bets, and he was the one usually sent out with the money to the bookie's office in the nearby town. On the face of it, de Valera seemed a curious choice for the other masters to have made, but perhaps they felt he could be trusted with their money!

In 1966 Eamon de Valera stood for election for the last time, when he was nominated for a second term of office as President of Ireland. He was now 84 years old, and it might have been expected that he would not run again. But this was the 50th anniversary of the Easter Rising, and it was thought that this would ensure the election of the 'last Commandant' of 1916. In fact he almost lost the election, beating Tom O'Higgins by only 10,000 out of a total of over one million votes cast. O'Higgins was not a particularly strong candidate, but he had one great advantage: he was more than 30 years younger than de Valera.

Little was said about de Valera's age during the campaign, though it was very much a factor in voters' minds. I even knew Fianna Fáil Cumann Secretaries who refused to work in the election. To campaign for a man who would be 91 if he completed his term of office was more than they were willing to do. Such attitudes, of course, were particularly strong in Dublin, where de Valera had never been popular. He carried the country, but lost heavily in Dublin, the biggest majority against him being in Dún Laoghaire-Rathdown. By chance, Seán Butler, Fianna Fáil Director of Elections in that constituency, met de Valera a couple of days later, and apologised for the dreadful result. 'Never mind, my boy,' said de Valera, 'the Dublin people were always very flighty.'

Seán Lemass

When Eamon de Valera resigned as Taoiseach in 1959, on his election as President of Ireland, no one was in any doubt that he would be succeeded by Seán Lemass. There were perhaps two others whose seniority was such that they might have been eligible to be considered. One of these was Seán MacEntee, who was not, I think, looked on as suitable by anyone in the Parliamentary Party, and who would in any event have been ruled out by his extreme unpopularity throughout the country. The other possibility was Dr James Ryan, who had no interest in the leadership, and was a strong backer of Lemass.

There may have been a few rural Deputies who would have preferred someone less closely linked to Dublin, but in the absence of any other possible candidate they had little if anything to say. Though I was not myself at that moment a member of the Parliamentary Party, I was in Leinster House on the day of the election of Seán Lemass as leader. I will always remember the sense of exhilaration that pervaded the place. For years the Fianna Fáil organisation, particularly the younger people, had been waiting and hoping for this day.

What were the qualities in Seán Lemass that roused such enthusiasm, not merely in the Parliamentary Party but throughout the Fianna Fáil organisation as a whole? He did not have the charisma of de Valera, nor had he been directly involved in the great political and constitutional advances of the 1930s. His contribution had been a different one, the bringing about of a transformation of Ireland's economy. To this he brought an endless flow of ideas and a dynamic approach that made him, after de Valera, the most prominent member of successive Fianna Fáil Governments. By the time Eamon de Valera retired, it was to Lemass that we all looked, to be the architect of the new Ireland that was emerging after World War II.

When de Valera formed the first Fianna Fáil Government in 1932 he gave Lemass the task – which indeed became his life's work – of creating in Ireland a modern industrial economy. It is sometimes forgotten today how unpromising the industrial climate was at the beginning of the 1930s. That was the period when each year in March advertisements were inserted in the newspapers, calling upon everyone during the week of St Patrick's Day to buy, if at all possible, one item manufactured in Ireland. As soon, therefore, as he became Minister for Industry and Commerce, Lemass instituted a complete system of protection, with imports of about 2,000 articles being made subject to tariffs or other restrictions. As a direct result, some 900 factories or workshops were set up in the seven years before the 'Emergency' ended progress. All these catered solely for the small home market.

On a larger scale, a number of State Companies were set up by Lemass that are still in existence today. These include Bord na Móna, the Irish Life Insurance Company, Irish Steel, Aer Lingus and the Irish Tourist Board (later Bord Fáilte). Under Lemass, the Department of Industry and Commerce dealt with many matters that are now covered by other Departments. He was therefore responsible for the development of Shannon Airport and the establishment of the Shannon Free Airport Development Company. He brought in Unemployment Assistance and Children's Allowances, and set up the Labour Court.

With this record it is not surprising that on the outbreak of the Second World War in 1939, he was given the key post of Minister for Supplies. This post was, Eamon de Valera said, to be the 'central planning department for our economic life.' Lemass had, in effect, unlimited powers to control imports, exports, prices, rationing, production and many other matters.

As an island country, neutral Ireland was in a difficult position; essential imports were in short supply, sometimes unobtainable. Lemass set up Irish Shipping Ltd, and second-hand ships were bought wherever possible in order to keep the country supplied. But there were never enough ships, and some were sunk, in spite of their neutral status. In one instance, after a tanker was sunk, the already small petrol ration had to be cut to just one-eighth of its former level. In fact, for the greater part of the 'Emergency' period, the petrol ration was given only to doctors and a very limited range of other people. The Dublin streets were almost deserted, and on one tour of the West of Ireland I cycled a distance of about 150 miles without meeting one motor car.

Everyone, obviously, rode a bicycle, but even here there were problems. When a headlight battery gave out, it was very difficult to find another: but that didn't stop the Gardaí from prosecuting those unfortunates without lights on their bikes. I remember an occasion when a law student – who later in life became a distinguished Ambassador – was cycling home one night in Dublin, without a light. As he reached Waterloo Road, still some miles from home, he noticed a Garda in the distance, and at once got off his bicycle. He realised though, that wheeling his bike on the road would still put him in trouble for not having a light. Were he to wheel it on the pavement, however, he would commit some different offence. So he threw the bicycle over his shoulder and set off along the pavement. He passed the Garda, who then turned and followed after him, about ten feet behind. As the unfortunate student at last turned in to the family gate, the Garda said 'Good night, Sir,' and turned back towards Dublin.

No domestic coal at all was available, and Seán Lemass organised an enormous campaign of turf production. The turf produced in this way was brought up to Dublin, and a stack about half a mile long was set up on the main road through the Phoenix Park. Each time it rained, of course, the turf got wetter, and the small ration tended to last a long time because of the great difficulty in getting it to burn.

Electricity was also heavily rationed, and in Dublin there was a special problem with gas, which was used by almost everyone for cooking. Here there was no specific ration, but the supply was cut off at 8 a.m., by which time breakfast was supposed to be finished; there was a further hour of gas at lunchtime, and then a couple of hours in the evening so that people could cook dinner. The problem was that the Gas Company had to keep some gas at all times in the pipes, to avoid explosions, so that it was possible to boil a kettle at any time of day on what became known as 'the glimmer'. To avoid this, the Company recruited a team of inspectors universally known as 'glimmermen'. The 'glimmerman' would come to the door (he had to be let in), and would head straight for the kitchen stove. He would put his hand on each of the gas rings, and if any one of them was hot the unfortunate consumer was cut off on the spot.

Perhaps the shortage that was most deeply felt was tea. The tea ration at first was two ounces a week, but for most of the 'Emergency' this was cut to a mere half ounce per week. I once heard Lemass explain how this happened. At the start of the War his Department began buying large quantities of tea in the Far East, for stock-piling purposes. The London tea merchants objected to this because, they said, the Department's activities were running up tea prices. If the Irish stopped buying tea, they said, they would guarantee to supply us with enough tea for the rest of the War to enable a two-ounce ration to be maintained. But they broke their promise.

It might have been expected that Seán Lemass, as the Minister responsible for the rationing system, would have become very unpopular – he was sometimes called 'Half-ounce Lemass'. But in fact his prestige rose during the 'Emergency' years because of the efficiency and obvious fairness with which the whole system was run. There were frequent and well-advertised prosecutions of those breaking the regulations, and however much people might complain, at least they knew that no one else was in a better position.

It is remarkable that Lemass was able to maintain his popularity in face of a whispering campaign of rumours that was directed against him. He had always been the subject of such rumours. It was alleged that he lost large sums of money, both at cards and also to bookies at the race track, and, indeed, was threatened with bankruptcy and had to be bailed out by rich industrialists. He was supposed to be engaged in all sorts of dubious business practices.

As Minister for Supplies, of course, he was the subject of further allegations. One day my mother was going in to town on a tram when she heard two women talking about Lemass. They knew 'for a fact' that two days earlier a load of six tons of the best coal had arrived at the Lemass house, and was at that very moment lying in the back garden. My mother thereupon broke into the conversation, pointing out that she lived three doors from Seán Lemass (in Palmerston Road), that from her top window she could see the whole of his back garden, and that there was no coal at all lying in it. But of course that kind of scandalmongering would normally go unrefuted.

A long time after the 'Emergency' had ended, I was approached in the Seanad by Senator William A. Sheldon, who said he would like to tell me a story about Seán Lemass. Sheldon was a Donegal Protestant, who for years had been a Dáil Deputy. He had traditionally voted against Fianna Fáil, until, to everyone's amazement, in 1952 he voted for MacEntee's severe Budget. No one knew at that stage if he was going to continue to support the Government – which was in a minority in the Dáil. A few weeks after that he went to see Lemass, to ask him to authorise the importation of a particular piece of machinery. This was required by Sheldon's most influential Donegal supporter, who claimed that it was vital for his business.

The importation of the item concerned was not subject to any specific regulation, but was entirely a matter for Lemass's personal decision. At a period of general scarcity, it was for the Minister for Industry and Commerce to hand out licences for imports, in accordance with his view of national needs. After Sheldon had put his case, Lemass said, in his usual gruff way: 'Right, I'll look into it. Come back next week.' So he came back a week later, and Lemass looked at him and said, 'Sorry Senator, can't be done.' Sheldon finished his story by saying, 'I left that room a much happier man than when I went in.'

Senator Sheldon intended in that story to demonstrate the absolute integrity of Seán Lemass; here was a Minister who was prepared to risk the life of the Government, rather than take a decision he believed to be wrong. But it tells us more than that. It underlines also the rigidity with which Lemass enforced the policies of his Department. I remember a meeting of the National Executive which was considering the list of names to be proposed at Constituency Conventions before the 1957 general election. They reached the name of an individual from a Border constituency, and someone asked, 'Wasn't he put in prison during the 'Emergency' for smuggling?' 'Oh,' asked de Valera, 'In or out?' 'Makes no difference', growled Lemass. So far as he was concerned, even though smuggling inwards might help to improve the country's supply position, it was still in breach of his Department regulations. In the end it was agreed that the person concerned was much too efficient a smuggler to travel 'light' in either direction. It was also felt, though, that he had now served his sentence and was entitled to run for election. He was duly elected, and spent some years in the Dáil, the terror of the Whips' Office, who could never find him when his vote was needed in a Dáil division.

Of all Lemass's years in office, his least effective period was probably the three years between 1951 and 1954. Fianna Fáil had come back to office having done nothing to renew their policies in the light of changing times; and that very conservative Minister for Finance, Seán MacEntee, was the dominant figure in the Cabinet. For the first time Lemass was reduced to a position of relative unimportance in Government.

He did take one important step: having strongly opposed the establishment of the Industrial Development Authority (IDA) by the previous Coalition Government, he now decided to keep it. It has now of course become one of the most effective arms of our industrial policy. I was listening one day to Lemass speaking in the Dáil about the IDA. He was interrupted by Gerard Sweetman of Fine Gael, who pointed out that he had previously opposed its establishment. 'All right,' said Lemass, 'so I've changed my mind. What about it?' That ended the argument. This was the only time I have ever heard a politician admit to having changed his mind: for some reason such an admission seems to be looked on as a confession of weakness to be avoided at all costs.

After losing the General Election of July, 1954, Fianna Fáil again went into opposition. Seán Lemass now became Director of Organisation, and settled in to Headquarters in Upper Mount Street. Since I was on the staff there (dealing with publicity), I was able to see at first hand the particular qualities of Lemass of which I had heard so much over the years.

He at once took on the task of renewing and revitalising Fianna Fáil, travelling the country with young members of the Organisation Committee, much as he had done thirty years earlier, when the Party was first set up. Very highly organised himself, he had a remarkable capacity to master a brief; in a short time he knew all there was to know about the state of the organisation in each Dáil constituency. Where there were weaknesses, they were dealt with. But this was not enough: he also wanted to know about any local political problems there might be all over the country. Each week, therefore, I read some 45 local newspapers and cut out for him to read any items that might possibly be of political interest. There might be a demand for a new hospital or school, a complaint about the condition of roads, a wrangle about the Chairmanship of a Council, a farmers' protest about the price of cattle, workers laid off at some local factory. All such items were grist to the Lemass mill.

His capacity for the taking of instant decisions could be disconcerting. During an election, for example, I might come in of a morning with a list of some 15 decisions that had to be made. I would mention them one by one, getting in each case a one-word or two-word reply. The whole thing would take about one minute, and that would be the end of it. He never went back on a decision, nor indeed did he ever ask whether an instruction had been carried out.

When Fianna Fáil went back into office in 1957 – this time with an overall majority – Lemass was back in the Department of Industry and Commerce, and Dr James Ryan became Minister for Finance. They both held the same general views on economic matters, and they backed Kenneth Whitaker (Secretary of the Department of Finance) when he produced his famous 'Integrated programme of national development.' Based on this, the 'Programme for Economic Expansion' was launched in 1958. This marked the beginning of a new drive for economic growth, and the end of the policy of protection, which had no relevance to post-War conditions.

Finally, in 1959, Seán Lemass became Taoiseach; many of us felt that he should have reached that position at least ten years earlier. He was now aged 60, and was to remain just seven years as Taoiseach. Now that he was at last in charge of affairs, he was able to press ahead with economic development without having to deal any longer with the difficulties and objections raised by other members of the Cabinet. For 21 years he had been a Minister under Eamon de Valera, who sought constantly for unanimity, however much this might delay the process of decision-making. Now Lemass could follow his own belief, which was that a rapid decision was better than inaction. If a mistake was made, then you could always make adjustments.

There could be no better example of this than the attitude he took at the time of Donogh O'Malley's celebrated announcement to the National Union of Journalists in September, 1966, that he proposed to introduce a scheme of free secondary education, beginning in September of the following year. O'Malley had no official authority for this announcement; he had no Government sanction, and Jack Lynch, as Minister for Finance, protested that he had not even been consulted. It is accepted, however, that Seán Lemass knew all about O'Malley's proposals, and that he may even have made changes in the text of his speech.

No Government decision would normally be taken on any matter with financial implications, until the views of the Department of Finance had been heard; and of course the O'Malley scheme raised all sorts of problems. An estimate had to be made of the number of extra pupils likely to take advantage of free secondary education. On this would depend the number and cost of the new or enlarged schools required and the number of extra teachers needed. There were numerous other financial questions, such as the number of school buses needed in rural areas. Past experience would suggest that O'Malley would have faced an endless series of objections from Finance.

Seán Lemass himself knew only too well, from his long years as Minister, the power wielded by the Department of Finance. The practical effect of his support for O'Malley was to by-pass the entire process of scrutiny by Finance, and to ensure in advance that the scheme would get immediate Government approval. No more public forum than the National Union of Journalists could have been chosen for such an announcement. At a time when more than 80 per cent of all children left school at the age of 14, the O'Malley proposals created a sensation and received a universal welcome. Whatever later criticisms Lemass may have made about the precise wording of O'Malley's speech, he knew very well that once the announcement had been made, there was no turning back.

Why did Lemass make such a break with normal Cabinet procedure? After all, as Taoiseach, he had all the authority he needed to ensure that the scheme was adopted. He could have overcome the delays and objections of the Department of Finance. The answer, I think may be a simple one. O'Malley's announcement of free secondary education was made in September 1966. In October 1966, just a few weeks later, Seán Lemass announced his intention to resign from the position of Taoiseach.

He had long had a deep interest in education and believed that it had the potential to make a much greater contribution to economic growth. My personal belief is that he determined, before his resignation, to ensure that the free secondary education scheme went through. After he had left the scene, there was no guarantee that this would happen – nor even that Donogh O'Malley would be left as Minister for Education. So the last act of Seán Lemass as Taoiseach was to empower O'Malley to transform the whole future of the young people of Ireland.

There is no knowing what Donogh might have achieved had he lived longer, with his flow of ideas and his bulldozing methods of getting his proposals through. Certainly he had begun taking an interest in the teaching of Irish in schools. I was once again a Senator, so I was present at a meeting of the Parliamentary Party at which this question was discussed. During the debate I gave the views I had long held with regard to the teaching of Irish as a spoken language, and Donogh O'Malley came to me afterwards and asked me to send these views to him in writing. I therefore sent him the following note:

> Herewith a summary of my views on the teaching of Irish in schools, which I promised to send you, after last week's Party meeting.
>
> 1. In assessing the effectiveness of any policy for the revival of Irish, the only real issue to be considered is – is the fluent *speaking* of Irish being fostered? It is, I think, universally accepted that the schools are not at the moment doing this: the national schools are not too bad, but the secondary schools are hopeless, with very few exceptions.
> 2. In the past the Department has, I think, been largely responsible for this state of affairs. It has tended to take the view that Irish must be taught as an academic subject; this involves a good deal of grammar, the learning of complicated poems off by heart, much reading of set books, etc. There is no

oral requirement for the Intermediate, and even the Leaving Certificate oral examination – with only 100 marks out of 600 – is inadequate (anyone getting even 48% on the Pass written paper could get no marks at all in the Oral and still pass).

3. I would urge that, if necessary, everything else should be sacrificed from the Irish course, in order to produce a new generation of fluent, natural Irish speakers. There should, I suggest, be a *Course in Spoken Irish* which every child in primary, secondary and vocational schools would have to take, whether they were doing Honours or not. This would be designed to ensure that from year to year the pupils' vocabulary and freedom of expression would steadily improve. As a matter of extreme urgency a completely new series of text books should be prepared, and full use made of tape recorders, gramophone records, Radio and Television, etc. Special training courses for teachers may be necessary.
4. In addition to the compulsory Course in Spoken Irish (which would be purely linguistic, and include no teaching of literature, etc.), there should also in all post-primary schools be an Honours course in Irish on similar lines to the course in use at present.
5. In other words, I am suggesting that every child, whether or not he or she chooses later on to follow an Honours Course, will, from at least the age of six to the time of leaving school, have had the benefit of an intensive, scientific, carefully graded course in the spoken language. But this must be simple and practical: it should on no account be academic. It would, I suggest, be fatal merely to add a course in spoken Irish to the existing written courses – or anything like them. The present system leads to a great deal of drudgery and heart-burning, with very poor results at the end of it all.

All good luck with your labours – you'll need it!

I have no idea what Donogh O'Malley made of all this. My memorandum set out a language policy that could have been tried out 30 years earlier, but I am not sure that it was still possible in the late 1960s. All prospect of any real change ended, however, with his sudden death after less than two years in charge of the Department of Education. But, I am sure that had he lived, he would have made some revolutionary reforms in the teaching of Irish.

Shortly after becoming Taoiseach, Seán Lemass had launched his new approach to Partition in his 'One Nation' speech. In the following years he developed this policy by gradually phasing out the use of the expression 'Six Counties', on the grounds that it was considered offensive by Unionists. This was the period when the *Sunday Press*, for example, threatened its journalists with instant suspension for using the expression 'Northern Ireland' in their articles.

In January 1965, Lemass made his celebrated visit to Belfast to visit Terence O'Neill in Stormont. This brief meeting may only have been a gesture, but it was a gesture that would not have been made by Eamon de Valera. It was a dramatic demonstration of the new approach that had been adopted by the Government. The visit was, I think, universally welcomed on our side of the Border. Certainly I heard of no one in the Fianna Fáil Party or the organisation generally who uttered the slightest objection.

When Lemass announced his intention to retire, it is strange that he should have done so without making any adequate provision for the succession. He does seem to have asked Jack Lynch whether he was interested in becoming Taoiseach, but accepted his answer when he denied interest. Had he been pushed, it is likely that Lynch would have agreed to run, just as on previous occasions he had (hesitantly) agreed to accept positions in the Cabinet. Not for nothing did he have the reputation of being a 'reluctant candidate'.

This unusually passive attitude of Lemass was quite unlike his normal positive approach to decision-making. It had the result that, once Jack Lynch had refused to run, this left a completely open field. The first two candidates to appear were Charles J. Haughey and George Colley. Both were in their early forties. Haughey had been in the Cabinet since 1961, first as an extremely effective Minister for Justice, and then as Minister for Agriculture. Colley had only 18 months Government experience; he was briefly Minister for Education after the 1965 election, and was then transferred to Industry and Commerce. Why then was he considered as a possible Taoiseach? I am not at all sure what the answer is to that question, though I do remember that in his short period as Minister for Education he had gained considerable prestige by standing up to Bishop Browne of

Galway, who had strongly opposed the Department's decision to close one- and two-teacher schools.

At this stage Neil Blaney of Donegal entered the field. He was just a little older than the other candidates, and he had been somewhat longer in Government. Lemass had chosen him as Minister for Local Government in 1959. He would not normally have been taken seriously as a possible Taoiseach. His manner was aggressive, his attitude belligerent, and his approach to politics was totally uncompromising. He was also extremely able; but there is no doubt that as Taoiseach he would have been a disaster. However, he would have sought support from the Party as the only candidate outside Dublin, and on that basis he might have done well amongst the rural Deputies.

At this stage the Parliamentary Party began to panic. In the 40 years since Fianna Fáil was founded there had never been a contest for the leadership, and this looked like becoming a particularly messy one. Various Deputies went to see Lemass, and he summoned Lynch again. This time he agreed to run. Haughey and Blaney thereupon withdrew, but Colley refused, and was beaten by 52 to 19. Jack Lynch therefore became leader of Fianna Fáil, a position he held for the next 13 years.

Seán Lemass remained in the Dáil until the 1969 election, and died just three years later. The enormous numbers at his State funeral were a tribute to a very great man. Certainly, for me, he was the politician whom I have most admired.

Without a Leader

Jack Lynch became Taoiseach in 1966 – exactly 40 years after the foundation of the Fianna Fáil organisation. The two giant figures of the past, de Valera and Lemass, had gone, and had now been replaced by an essentially ordinary man. Lynch did not have the seniority of his predecessors, nor their historic links with the early days of the national movement. He had emerged as leader of Fianna Fáil because he was a few years older than the other candidates, was extremely popular with the general public, and had the longest experience in Government. In the course of his ministerial career he had never excited controversy: it may be that as a former civil servant he had absorbed the civil service creed that the best way to keep out of trouble is to refrain from taking decisions until they become unavoidable. Lynch was not an 'ideas' man. In his various ministries he proved to be a competent administrator, but it is hard to remember any initiatives that he took while in office.

His great problem in his early years as Taoiseach was that he had in his Cabinet several people who were more able, more ambitious and more energetic than he was. Perhaps the most prominent of these was Charles Haughey. For 30 years Haughey was a dominant figure in Irish public life, but during his entire political career he has been involved in controversy. Now in his retirement he has become a tragic and discredited figure, having admitted that while in office as Taoiseach he accepted enormous payments from business sources for his personal use. It is this that will always remain in people's minds when they think of Charles Haughey. Yet he should also go down in history as a brilliantly successful Minister.

The list of items of beneficial legislation brought in by him during his Ministerial career is a very long one. In the field of legal reform, he did a great deal to modernise the entire legal system. Amongst this mass of legislation was the Succession Act (laying down that testators must provide adequately for their families in their wills), the introduction of free legal aid and the effective abolition of the death penalty.

The most controversial item introduced by Haughey was the Family Planning Bill. Two previous attempts to introduce such a Bill had failed; on the second occasion the then Taoiseach, Liam Cosgrave, voted against his own Government's Bill. During the debate in the Seanad early in 1979, in speaking in favour of Haughey's very restrictive Bill I pointed out that it was a first step – that after previous failures the one essential was to get some kind of Bill through. During an interval in the debate I said to Haughey that of course the restrictions in his Bill were ridiculous, but that once the principle had been established that contraception was legal, then it would presumably be possible later on to liberalise its provisions. He made no objection to this proposition. But in fact he opposed the amending Bill brought in six years later by the FitzGerald Coalition, designed to widen the scope of his own 1979 Act.

In the health field Haughey brought in the first free hospitalisation scheme, and speeded up the provision of new hospitals. He took extensive powers to control the advertising of tobacco products; at a meeting with the tobacco companies he was asked for the words of warning that they were going to have to use on their products. He said 'smokers die younger', upon which there was a general, rather nervous, laugh: he had to explain that he was serious, it was not a joke.

Haughey also brought in a number of schemes for the benefit of Old Age Pensioners: free travel, free TV licences and free telephone rental. Finally, he introduced a unique measure that has created a great deal of interest abroad, complete freedom from income tax for writers and artists on their earnings from creative work.

If Charles Haughey was the most imaginative and effective of the Ministers who served under Jack Lynch, there were several other strong-minded individuals included in his various Cabinets. Of these, the most prominent was Neil Blaney, who had been Minister for Local Government since 1957, and was moved to Agriculture by Jack Lynch.

He accomplished little in Agriculture, following the example of his predecessor in the Department (Charlie Haughey) by getting involved in an acrimonious row with the agricultural organisations. In Local Government he was responsible for the scheme to bring piped water to the homes of rural Ireland. Everyone now accepts that this scheme was one of the great factors in raising the standard of living amongst country dwellers; but it was not always so. During a Seanad election in 1961 I was present one day at a meeting of Leitrim County Council, to find several hundred angry farmers holding a meeting outside. They were protesting at the extravagance of Councillors, who were proposing to spend large sums of the ratepayers' money on 'unnecessary' water schemes. I don't think that any of the protestors had brought their wives with them; they were probably at home trekking across the fields to get a bucket of water from the local well!

Blaney's main interest while dealing with Local Government was the provision of much needed housing in Dublin. He realised that Dublin Corporation was quite incapable of meeting the need for houses, and so he decided that the Department itself would construct a new town at Ballymun. I remember well the enthusiasm with which he talked of the scheme, and of all the families who would be housed there. Ballymun of course turned out to be a disaster, and now, 30 years later, the whole place is to be torn down and a new start made. Blaney himself always maintained that Ballymun was never finished as he had envisaged it. He blamed Kevin Boland, his successor in the Department, for giving up all control over the scheme, simply handing it over to the Housing Department of the Corporation.

Over the years any Senator or Deputy can get a good idea of the competence of Ministers from the manner in which they pilot legislation through the House. Of all the Ministers that I observed at this task during the 22 years I spent in the Seanad, Neil Blaney was perhaps the ablest, with an amazing grasp of his brief. I remember one occasion when he was dealing with the Committee stage of a long and complicated Local Government Bill. For several hours he went through the Bill section by section, amendment by amendment (there was a large number), answering all questions. He had no notes, and never once consulted with the civil service experts who accompanied him. On the other hand, he refused to accept even one single amendment. In each case he explained in detail why he was rejecting the amendment, but that cannot have been much consolation to Senators on the Opposition benches. This total inflexibility was his greatest fault as a Minister.

Blaney was perhaps best known as an organiser. He fought countless by-elections, bringing to these a tireless energy and a 1930s style of campaigning that he had learned as a child in Donegal. He and Kevin Boland shared out the by-elections between them. Boland (as he explained to me once at an election in Waterford) would be sent to deal with the quieter type of constituency, while Blaney would descend on the more traditional areas in Connacht and elsewhere. He would arrive with a group of his Donegal party workers – universally known as the 'Donegal mafia' – and the voters would be exposed to an endless series of public meetings, torchlight parades, bonfires of burning motor tyres and general excitement. In the right place all this could be very effective; in the wrong place things could go wrong. Blaney ran the Fianna Fáil campaign in Limerick City that put Des O'Malley into the Dáil on the sudden death of his uncle Donogh. O'Malley – and perhaps others of the citizenry of Limerick – complained about the nature of the Blaney campaign, in particular the painting of walls with provocative slogans.

Neil Blaney was a magnificent orator, in the barn-storming style. I remember his being sent in once at a Fianna Fáil Árd- Fheis to deal with a motion that had the backing of the great majority of delegates but was opposed by the National Executive. After half an hour the sheer intensity of his oratory was such that his audience erupted in a storm of applause, and voted almost unanimously against the motion that they had come to Dublin to support.

In the early Lynch years Blaney came to be associated in the public mind in particular with Kevin Boland, though in fact they only had one thing in common: they considered themselves to be the last true 'Republicans' left in Fianna Fáil. In all other respects, however, they were entirely different. Where Blaney, with all his faults, was an extremely able Minister, Boland was an essentially mediocre figure. He first came to office under curious circumstances, when Fianna Fáil returned to power in 1957. Kevin's father, Gerald Boland, had been a Minister for many years, a founder of Fianna

Fáil and a close associate of Eamon de Valera. When told that he would not be a member of the new Government, he reacted so strongly that de Valera agreed to replace him with his son Kevin, who thus became a Minister on his first day in the Dáil.

I am afraid that I have no memory at all of anything achieved by Kevin Boland in the first ten years of his membership of the Cabinet. I cannot even remember what Ministries he held, though in his favour it must be said that he has always been painfully honest and sincere. It was in connection with the 1968 Referendum on Proportional Representation (PR) that, for the first time, Boland made an impact as a member of the Government. It was his task, as Minister for Local Government, to draft the legislation leading up to the Referendum.

I have never been able to understand why it was decided to hold this Referendum, nor indeed who initiated the idea. Only a few years earlier, in 1959, the first attempt to abolish PR had failed. At that time it had been hoped to increase the chances of success in the Referendum by holding it on the same day as the election in which Eamon de Valera was running for the Presidency. He was indeed elected by a large majority, but a large number of those who voted for him voted against the proposal to abolish Proportional Representation. Now it was proposed to start all over again, but this time without the advantage of staging the Referendum alongside the de Valera election campaign.

There may have been a few Ministers who believed the 1968 Referendum could be won, but I don't believe there was anyone else in the Parliamentary Party who thought we had a chance. There was a long and vigorous debate. I proposed an amendment to the effect that we should preserve the existing single transferable vote, but in single member constituencies – the same system as is used at Dáil by-elections. There was a reasonable chance that Fine Gael might agree to this, and it might well have been more acceptable to the general public than the 1959 'straight vote' proposal had been.

There was a lot of support for my amendment amongst Deputies and Senators, but from the solid Ministerial block there was not a breath of compromise: they were political lemmings, heading for the nearest cliff. A large majority of those who spoke in the debate were opposed to the holding of a new Referendum, but in the end only seven of us voted against. So we were launched into a struggle that all of us knew was hopeless. As the Minister immediately concerned, Kevin Boland bore the brunt of the campaign. In the Seanad on the Second Stage of the Referendum Bill, he spoke for six and a half hours, at the end of which he said that he had a lot more to say, but that Senators on the Opposition benches seemed to be rather tired. There was a long campaign, with much use (and abuse) of statistics, but in the end, as was inevitable, the proposal was heavily defeated. I hope that one day some historian will find out who was responsible for persuading the Cabinet to embark on this totally futile campaign.

Jack Lynch's first General Election as Taoiseach took place in 1969. The Fianna Fáil vote was down by 2 per cent, perhaps due to the unpopularity of the previous year's Referendum. However, they gained three seats and an overall majority, due to a refusal by the Labour Party to co-operate with Fine Gael in the mutual exchange of preferences.

Yet in spite of the success in the election, Jack Lynch was steadily losing control of his Government. Even before the election, Neil Blaney in a speech quite contrary to Government policy on the North had, amongst other things, described the harmless Stormont Prime Minister, Terence O'Neill, as a bigot. Lynch took no action to deal with this defiance. When he was forming his new Government he was again defied by Blaney, who refused point blank to accept a new position as Minister for Planning. Lynch was forced therefore to leave him in the Department of Agriculture.

Neil Blaney was not so successful in another, less important field. Liam Ó Buachalla for many years had been Cathaoirleach (Chairman) of the Seanad, but had retired at the 1969 election. I was asked to stand in his place for the position of Cathaoirleach, and agreed to run. Another candidate appeared, John J. Nash, a solicitor from Templemore, County Tipperary.

Since Fianna Fáil were in Government, they had a majority in the Seanad, so that their choice for Cathaoirleach would automatically be accepted by the 60 Senators. The decision therefore would be made at a meeting of the Fianna Fáil Seanad group of some 31 members. This matter was of course of interest to Senators; there was a certain prestige involved in being Cathaoirleach. But the position had no political importance, and the choice of a Cathaoirleach had never roused any particular excitement outside the immediate ranks of the Senators. Certainly no Dáil Deputy had ever taken any part in the proceedings.

On this occasion things were different. On the day before the Fianna Fáil Senators were to meet to choose their candidate, Neil Blaney suddenly intervened. He began summoning the various Senators to his ministerial office in Leinster House, and then instructed them – in his typically over-bearing style – that they must vote for Nash and not for Yeats. Thereupon Brian Lenihan and Charlie Haughey emerged from their own offices and went through Leinster House urging Fianna Fáil Senators to vote for me. At the Seanad group meeting next day I got through fairly easily, and in due course became Cathaoirleach – one of the very few such occasions when Neil Blaney did not get his way. But I have never understood why he got involved at all. There did not seem to be any reason why he should be interested in John Nash, a smooth professional man of extremely conservative instincts, and in no sense a 'Republican' in Blaney's sense of the term. On the other hand, so far as I was concerned, I could not think of any reason why Neil should want to prevent me becoming Cathaoirleach, a position in which he had not previously shown the slightest interest. It was a mystery.

In August 1969, serious street-fighting broke out in Belfast and Derry, with attacks on Catholic homes by Orange mobs, in some cases with help from members of the RUC. An urgent Government meeting was held, and on the same night the Taoiseach spoke on Television, warning that 'The Irish Government can no longer stand by and see innocent people injured.' This, however, was not Jack Lynch's speech. His own draft was rejected as too mild by his colleagues in Government, and what finally emerged was a text produced by them collectively, and given to him to read. At that crucial moment in our history Jack Lynch was no longer the leader, merely a figurehead, a situation that led directly to the 'Arms Crisis' of the following year.

The origins and details of this whole affair are sunk in obscurity, but a few things are clear. There was a real fear amongst Nationalists in Northern

Ireland that in the absence of a neutral police force on which they could rely, their homes, perhaps their lives, were under threat. There was no Provisional IRA in existence, there were no arms with which the Nationalist people could defend themselves. A whole series of deputations from 'Citizens' Defence Committees' came to Dublin, seeking arms from the Irish Government. Included amongst their members were such eminently respectable pillars of society as Gerry Fitt, who has since become a member of the British House of Lords.

That much is established fact. It is also a fact that an attempt was made to import arms secretly so that they could be sent north to Belfast. I am no better informed than anyone else (other than those immediately involved) about just what took place. But over the years I have gained a strong impression that those trying to import the arms genuinely thought that in this activity they were carrying out Government policy, or that at the very least Jack Lynch knew about what they were doing. What is certain is that the Taoiseach had lost control of his Government, resulting in a period of almost total confusion.

No one, either inside or outside the Government, had any real idea of what to do about the Northern situation. Blaney and perhaps one or two others were calling for the Army to cross the Border in Derry or Armagh. The theory was that such an invasion would result in immediate United Nations intervention. Nothing immediate, of course, ever happens at the UN, and in any event Britain would have vetoed any such suggestion. In the meantime, what would have happened to the 100,000 Catholics cut off in Belfast City? But in the face of such lunatic suggestions Jack Lynch himself seemed to have nothing coherent to offer.

Even when Lynch was directly informed by Peter Berry (Secretary of the Department of Justice) of the attempt to import arms, he still did nothing. In the end, he only acted when the leader of Fine Gael, Liam Cosgrave, told him that he knew about the affair. Blaney and Haughey were immediately dismissed from the Government, and Lynch sent the papers to the Attorney General so that they could be prosecuted. The prosecutions failed. Míchéal Ó Móráin, Minister for Justice, had previously been forced by Lynch to resign as he was ill and clearly unable to deal with his Department. A fourth senior Minister, Kevin Boland, now resigned in

*Georgie [George] Hyde-Lees whom W.B. Yeats married in 1917.
This photograph of Michael Yeats' mother was taken c. 1920.*

W.B. Yeats with Anne and Michael, in a field at Ballylee, near Gort in Co. Galway.

Ballylee as it was in 1925. The Yeats family spent part of each year here until 1927.

A copy of the famous 'Dublin Opinion' cartoon (c.1925) showing the two absent-minded poets, W.B. Yeats and George Russell (AE), passing in the street on their way to visit each other's house. (see p. 34)

'L'Aple Fleurie' in Villars-sur-Bex, the school in Switzerland which Michael attended from 1927–30.

W.B. Yeats playing croquet with his daughter, Anne, at 'Riversdale', c. 1935.

W.B. Yeats pictured here in full flight during a BBC broadcast in 1936.

Brian Faulkner and Michael Yeats on O'Connell Bridge c. 1940.

Professor T.W. Moody, Eamon de Valera, T.C. Kingsmill Moore ('Visitor' to the University) and Michael Yeats, pictured in Trinity College, November 1944.

Teaċ An Ċustaim (Custom House) — Baile Áṫa Cliaṫ (Dublin)

F o r e w o r d

By Dr. NOEL C. BROWNE, Minister for Health

S U R E L Y it is our duty, as a nation based on the principles of justice and Christianity, to do our utmost to save the mothers and children of our race from avoidable disease and death.

I am resolved in the new Mother and Child Scheme to lay the foundation of a medical service which in time will avert suffering and bereavement from young families, as far as that is humanly possible.

This Booklet describes the coming Service, and explains the way in which we intend to work. When the Service is fully developed, all our mothers who choose to avail themselves of the scheme will have at their disposal for themselves and their children all the resources of modern medicine. This will be theirs as a right of their nationhood, and without any mark of the Poor Law, or any means test.

Let me stress the fact that the whole Scheme is voluntary. Neither in regard to the mothers and children, will there be any compulsion.

My authority for this Service is the will of our people, unmistakably expressed through the Oireachtas in the Health Act of 1947, which the former administration passed, and which the present Government endorses. Such authority none may refute.

The clear will of our people, guaranteeing equality of opportunity in matters of health and healing, has been my guide. I am sure that the comprehensive plan, here broadly outlined, will give effect to that will.

Aire Sláinte.

The Foreword from one of the information booklets that Dr Noel Browne (Minister for Health) continued to circulate even after his Coalition Government colleagues had rejected his 'Mother and Child' Scheme.

Michael Yeats with Oscar Traynor (then Minister for Justice), Eamon de Valera and Joe Groome. (Hon. Secretary of Fianna Fáil) c. 1954.

Michael and Anne Yeats on the bridge beside Ballylee, June 13, 1965. The tower, restored by Bord Fáilte, was opened to the public on that date – the centenary of the poet's birth.

Delivering the opening speech for the Irish delegation at the European Parliament in January, 1973.

Jim Gibbons, Brian Lenihan and Michael Yeats chatting with a French MEP at a 1975 meeting in Corsica.

Michael and Gráinne Yeats with Jack Lynch at a European Progressive Democrat Group meeting in 1975.

On an official visit to Ireland in May, 1975, Georges Spénale, President of the European Parliament (centre), is greeted by Senator James Dooge (then Cathaoirleach of the Seanad). Michael Yeats is on the left.

At the 1975 ACP Parliamentary Conference in Abidjan, in the Ivory Coast.

Addressing a Greek Management Association conference in Athens in 1975. George Colley is on the extreme right.

Presiding at a plenary session of the European Parliament.

Michael Yeats greets President Hillery on the occasion of his official visit to Luxembourg in September, 1978.

sympathy with Blaney and Haughey, though he had nothing to do with the importation of arms.

Jack Lynch had now been nominal leader of Fianna Fáil for four years; he was to remain for a further nine years, but under very different circumstances. Blaney and Boland were soon out of the Organisation; Haughey remained on, but was very much out in the cold. The Taoiseach could at last begin to assert the dominance that should normally go with that position. There was a state of utter confusion in Fianna Fáil about just what had been going on, but on one thing almost everyone agreed. Jack Lynch was the elected leader and, as such, was entitled to support at all levels of the Organisation.

With sometimes ruthless efficiency, for the first time he asserted his control, and when the next General Election came along, in 1973, he was able to campaign with a united Party behind him. It was a reflection of his great popularity that Fianna Fáil increased its share of the poll. This time, however, Fine Gael and Labour had issued a joint election manifesto, resulting in a much closer co-operation in the election and, as a result, a number of extra seats. After 16 years Fianna Fáil were out of office, and a Fine Gael/Labour Coalition Government was formed by Liam Cosgrave.

Cosgrave Coalition

The four years (1973–77) of the Coalition Government led by Liam Cosgrave marked a period of considerable change in my political career. Since 1969 I had been Cathaoirleach of the Seanad, a position from which I resigned on 1 January 1973, in order to accept a nomination to be one of the Fianna Fáil members of the European Parliament. Under the rules then applying to the Parliament I remained a Senator, and here also there was a big change. Before the 1973 General Election I had spent 15 years in the Seanad, and for all of that time Fianna Fáil were in Government. The main function in life of a Government Senator, of course, was to defend any Minister who came in with legislation – no matter how unreasonable that Minister might be. You could not even put down an amendment unless you were sure it was going to be accepted; otherwise the Opposition could call for a division and make you vote against your own amendment, thereby looking very foolish.

As Cathaoirleach, I no longer took part in debates: but in all the years before that, while speaking frequently, I was able to put down just one amendment, and that was to a Private-member's Bill that came to us from the Dáil. Paddy Smith (Minister for Local Government) accepted the Bill moved by Deputy Jack McQuillan of Roscommon, which proposed to empower local authorities to take over certain private roads. This was a useful piece of legislation, and everyone agreed with it, but I noticed an error in one section, which had the effect that a local authority was empowered to take over even a householder's front drive. I drafted an amendment to correct this error, and went off to Paddy Smith with it. I spent nearly an hour trying to persuade him, but I could not get him to see the point. Finally he turned to the Department officials who were with him and asked them what they thought. 'That is what we have been saying all along,' they said. But that was the only occasion in those frustrating years that I was able to have an amendment made to legislation.

Now that we were in Opposition, the next four years in the Seanad were busy ones, particularly since we had only a small number in the Fianna Fáil Group who had to cover a number of long and complicated items of legislation. The Seanad has a total of 60 members: at the start of the Coalition Government, in 1973, Fianna Fáil had 17 Senators, but we ended up in 1977 with just 13. This was due to an unusual number of by-elections. Under the peculiar rules governing Seanad elections, the vote in a by-election is limited to Senators and Deputies, so the Government always wins. The Opposition, however, can sometimes have a limited influence, as was the case in one of these by-elections in 1975. This was on the Agricultural Panel, and a number of farmer candidates had been nominated by the various Nominating Bodies. Of these, four were members of Fine Gael and would get full Government backing. One of the four, therefore, would inevitably be elected.

We discussed this matter at the Parliamentary Party, and it was pointed out that few of the Dublin Deputies and Senators would have much personal interest in the various Fianna Fáil candidates on the Agricultural Panel – none of whom of course could be elected. So it was agreed that we Dubliners would vote for the 'most useless' of the Fine Gael hopefuls. I should explain that this term had nothing to do with a candidate's abilities as a legislator. The only matter of concern was the extent to which a new Fine Gael Senator might be useful to his Party at local level in his constituency. As to which of the Fine Gael candidates was the 'most useless', no immediate decision could be reached, so a sub-committee was set up to consider this interesting question. After a week they came back with a name, a number of us voted for him, and in due course – no doubt much to his surprise – Senator Codd joined the Fine Gael Group. This must have been the only occasion in history that a candidate in a Seanad election actually got more votes than had been promised him.

The Coalition Government had barely settled in before a Presidential election took place in May 1973, on the ending of Eamon de Valera's term of office. Erskine Childers was the Fianna Fáil candidate, opposed by Tom

O'Higgins, who had almost defeated de Valera in 1966. Because he had previously done so well, Fine Gael were confident of victory, but in fact Childers won fairly easily. The speeches I heard him make were largely incomprehensible, but I think it was felt that a President should be somewhat above ordinary plain people. Nor did the voters worry about his anglified accent. Brian Lenihan, his Campaign Manager, used to tell hilarious stories about events on the Presidential bus. They would be passing through a small town where the local supporters had been brought out to cheer, and after unavailing efforts to get the candidate to wave back, Brian would take hold of Erskine's arm and flap it up and down in a sort of royal wave.

Once elected, Childers proved an extremely popular President, far more active and accessible than any of his predecessors. It was known, however, that there had been difficulties between him and the Taoiseach, Liam Cosgrave, though the precise nature of the disputes was not made public. According to the (Fine Gael) researcher Jim Duffy – writing in 1990 in *The Irish Times* – there were two specific problems that arose. Speaking personally, I had always assumed that the Cosgrave Government was invariably in the wrong in its dealings with President Childers, but it seems that on the two occasions mentioned by Duffy, Cosgrave's attitude was correct. It all goes to show that one should never take things for granted, especially where one's political prejudices are involved.

The first dispute stemmed from a Presidential proposal to set up a policy 'think-tank', a typically unrealistic Childers idea. He should have realised that it is none of a President's business to put forward policies on social or economic issues.

The second dispute, it seems, related to the President's wish to launch a fund-raising appeal for St Patrick's Cathedral in Dublin. My first reaction on reading Jim Duffy's *Irish Times* article was to think 'why not?': a President belonging to the 3 per cent Church of Ireland minority raising money for that tiny minority's Cathedrals. Then I thought, but what if, say, President de Valera had launched an appeal for the building of a Catholic Cathedral in Dublin? It would have been considered by many a clear breach of the separation of Church and State, a denial of the concept that the President is President for *all* the Irish people.

In the event, Erskine Childers died suddenly in November 1974, after only 18 months in office, cutting short what might have been a really great Presidency. Nobody wanted another Presidential election, particularly one so close to Christmas. Stephen Collins, in his recent book *The Cosgrave Legacy*, says that discussions took place between Jack Lynch and Liam Cosgrave about an agreed candidate to succeed Childers. Collins quotes Peter Barry as saying that the two of them came up with a list including the names of Rita Childers, the late President's widow, and Cearbhall Ó Dálaigh. According to Barry, 'Cosgrave told us at a Cabinet meeting on a Friday morning that he had discussed the matter with Lynch and that Rita Childers was acceptable.'

It is in fact almost inconceivable that Lynch would have preferred Mrs Childers to Ó Dálaigh, who was an infinitely more distinguished person; a former Chief Justice, he was now a member of the European Court in Luxembourg. In addition, from a party political point of view one could hardly forget that in earlier years he had been a Fianna Fáil Dáil candidate and Attorney General. Knowing Jack Lynch's form, I can imagine him sitting there during his discussions with Liam Cosgrave, smoking his pipe and conveying an impression of agreement, but without in fact saying anything. This was a characteristic of his that caused difficulties on other occasions during his political career.

The question of the succession to Erskine Childers was in fact discussed at a meeting of the Fianna Fáil Parliamentary Party. Early in the discussion one of the younger Deputies brought up the name of Rita Childers. He referred to all the support she was getting in the media, suggested that she would be a very strong candidate and that, campaigning on a wave of sympathy, she might well be unbeatable. Perhaps, therefore, we should agree to her nomination.

I stood up immediately and opposed this very strongly: we in Fianna Fáil should not agree to this under any circumstances. I pointed out that the President was our first citizen. The office was of great symbolic importance, and should be filled only by people who had achieved real national distinction. I urged that Mrs Childers was in no way qualified as a possible Presidential candidate; she had simply been married to the late President.

I suggested that no other democratic country would elect someone to such a high office simply on the basis that she was a President's widow. If we were to do so, then we would become a laughing stock abroad. It might well be, I said, that under the existing circumstances she would be an unbeatable candidate. But even if we knew that 95 per cent of the votes would go to her, we would still have to put up a qualified candidate and accept the electoral defeat that might ensue. Perhaps I should add that even after 20 years I still have a precise memory of what I said, because of the strength of my feelings on the matter.

This view of the position was accepted by the entire Party. No other member spoke in favour of nominating Mrs Childers; her name was not even mentioned during the rest of the discussion. Jack Lynch himself at no time said a word about possible candidates. If he had indeed been thinking of agreeing to her nomination, then he now had to reconsider. He would have to accept that under no circumstances would his Parliamentary Party agree to such a proposal. In the event the agreed candidate was Cearbhall Ó Dálaigh, whose Presidency ended a year later with the fiasco in October, 1976, when the Minister for Defence, Paddy Donegan, accused him of being a 'thundering disgrace.' This was because Ó Dálaigh – in accordance with his rights under the Constitution – had referred an Offences Against the State Amendment Bill to the Supreme Court. When Liam Cosgrave refused to dismiss Donegan the President resigned in protest. Thus the Cosgrave Coalition had the unique experience of having to deal with four Presidents in succession: de Valera, Childers, Ó Dálaigh, and finally Dr Patrick Hillery.

There is one last thing that should be said about Mrs Rita Childers. A year after Erskine's death she was invited by Fianna Fáil to a mass for him and for other deceased Party Deputies. She refused in an extraordinary public statement, saying that 'the late President would not benefit from the prayers of such a party. Happily for him he is now closer to God, and will be able to ask His intercession that his much loved country will never again be governed by these people.' All I can say about this is that, had Mrs Childers succeeded in becoming President, she would have had great difficulty in remaining above politics, let alone conducting herself as President for *all* the Irish people.

On the formation of the Coalition in February 1973, Liam Cosgrave appointed as his Minister for Foreign Affairs Garret FitzGerald, who had been a Deputy for less than four years. He first appeared in the public eye when he began writing weekly articles on economic affairs in *The Irish Times*, around the year 1960. These were well-written, informative and to my mind surprising, in that more often than not they favoured the policies being carried out by the Fianna Fáil Government under Seán Lemass. My surprise was due to the fact that in all my years of reading *The Irish Times*, I could never remember a columnist with a favourable attitude to Fianna Fáil.

In conversations I had with Garret in the very early 1960s, it became clear that he had a great admiration for Seán Lemass. In fact, he told me one day that he would like to become a member of Fianna Fáil. I wondered what I should do about this; should I bring it to the notice of someone in party headquarters? In the end I decided to do nothing. It did not seem to me that he was interested in joining as an ordinary Cumann member: he would, I thought, expect instant nomination as Senator or Deputy. With no previous political experience, and with a Fine Gael rather than a Fianna Fáil background, I simply could not visualise him being pushed forward so rapidly.

Some years later I mentioned this conversation to the late Seán Flanagan, who said that he himself had the same experience, when Garret came to lunch one day at his house in Clontarf. There was the same expression of admiration for Lemass and the same suggestion that Garret would like to join Fianna Fáil. But like myself, Seán Flanagan brought the matter no further, presumably for similar reasons to my own. FitzGerald's flirtation with Fianna Fáil did not last long; inside three years he had joined Fine Gael. He became a Senator in 1965, a Deputy in 1969, and within a few years he had his ambitious eye on the leadership of Fine Gael.

By the time the 1973 Cosgrave Coalition was formed, Ireland had joined the EEC and I myself was a member of the European Parliament. I could therefore see at first hand the energy and efficiency that Garret FitzGerald brought to his work as Minister for Foreign Affairs. I am not sure, however, whether his overall influence on the Cosgrave Coalition was a helpful one. One of his great faults was that his approach to politics was often theoretical rather than practical. He had little real concept of public opinion, but relied on opinion polls to tell him what people were thinking.

Although a trained economist, Garret's judgement on financial matters was sometimes faulty. I came across one example of this first hand when Richie Ryan – as Minister for Finance – came into the Seanad early in 1975 with a Bill to introduce a Wealth Tax. This had been wished on a reluctant Fine Gael by the Labour Party, urged on in this instance by Garret FitzGerald.

The Bill proposed that everyone should each year make a list of all their possessions, and pay a tax of 1 per cent of their total value. It was a tax that would have been impossible to enforce because of its complexity, and was calculated to cause a maximum of irritation for a minimum of revenue. The only exemption from this tax was to be the 'principal dwelling house and normal contents.' What are normal contents, I asked the Minister? Furnishings brought in for investment purposes would be taxable, came the answer. What about a Persian carpet, or an antique dining room table, or a painting by Picasso on the wall? How could anyone possibly tell whether the householder had placed these in his home because he liked such things, or because he had bought them for later re-sale at a profit? I got no answer, not because Richie Ryan was at fault, but because there could be no answer. The Wealth Tax would have been a tax lawyer's Paradise.

At the same time that we were debating the Wealth Tax in 1975, Conor Cruise-O'Brien, Minister for Posts and Telegraphs, spent three months with us with a Broadcasting Bill. This was a curious piece of legislation that one would not have expected to see put forward by a member of an Irish Government. Its main provision gave the Minister power to force the RTÉ. Authority to use its second Television Channel for the purpose of broadcasting BBC 1 in its entirety. In other words, there were to be no Irish programmes whatever on our second TV service.

In the Seanad debate, I cross-examined Cruise-O'Brien about his precise intentions in this legislation. My reading of the Bill, I said, was that on Irish Television we were to get the BBC from the display of the Test Card in early morning to the playing each night of 'God Save the Queen' by the Grenadier Guards (or whomever), with a film of the Queen of England in uniform on her white horse, the Union Jack flapping behind. Cruise-O'Brien – this Irish Government Minister – told me that I was correct, that under the powers given to him in the Bill he proposed to instruct the RTÉ Authority to use their new second channel in precisely that manner.

In addition, Cruise-O'Brien in his Bill deleted the obligation that until then had been laid on RTÉ:

> *In performing its functions, the Authority shall bear constantly in mind the national aims of restoring the Irish language and preserving and developing the national culture and shall endeavour to promote the attainment of those aims.*

He explained in the Seanad why he was making this change. These two main concepts – restoring the Irish language, and preserving and developing the national culture – were not, he claimed, acceptable to many people in Ireland. In order to understand Cruise-O'Brien's thinking on this Bill, one needs to remember that in 1975 he was nearing the end of his political transformation from youthful radical to Unionist. In the following years he developed a stage further, returning to active politics as a member of the fringe UK Unionist Party, whose policies, on occasion, made Ian Paisley seem like a moderate.

Another controversial figure who appeared in the Seanad during the Coalition years was James Tully, Minister for Local Government. The controversy was not always caused by the actual content of the legislation that he brought before us; in fact the biggest row I have ever seen in the Seanad was in connection with a substantial yet perfectly harmless and routine Bill. It concerned local elections that were due to take place a few weeks later. The row was caused simply by Ministerial arrogance.

It is certainly true that all Governments, from time to time, treat the Seanad with some disdain. There are always some Ministers who look upon their appearance in the Upper House as a chore, and who may use procedural devices to shorten debate. But Jim Tully went far beyond anything of this kind that had ever been done before, at least in my memory. Senators were summoned by telegram to meet at 10.30 a.m. on 15 May, 1974, and were then told that the Local Elections Bill was to be passed through all stages by 2.30 p.m. that afternoon. Naturally we protested, pointing out that the Bill had first been introduced into the Dáil over a year before. We asked, without ever getting an answer, what had the Minister been doing with the Bill over all those months?

With our few Fianna Fáil Senators there was little we could do about this, except to make fiery speeches about Parliamentary democracy. We also, of course, used every possible procedural device to slow the Parliamentary juggernaut. At one stage Brendan Halligan (leader of the Labour Group) described me as an 'elegant butcher' – he assured me later on in private that this was meant as a compliment. I felt that in that case I must hope never to be insulted by him! In the end, we did manage to delay the enactment of the Bill by a couple of hours. Our efforts were an exercise in futility, but they may have been worthwhile, if only to discourage other Ministers from trying the same game.

I doubt, in fact, if any Minister today would dare to put on such a performance. Both Houses of the Oireachtas are now broadcast both on Television and Radio. The spectacle of the Upper House being called together by telegram and then given just four hours to enact all stages of a Bill – in the absence of a national emergency – would certainly have an impact on public opinion. Back in 1974 there were newspaper reporters present, but I do not remember any media comment on the affair. Television certainly has its faults, but it can be a great safeguard of Parliamentary democracy.

Later on we had a further visit by Jim Tully, with his notorious Bill to 'Tullymander' the Dáil constituencies. His general aim was to place three-seat constituencies wherever Fianna Fáil were weak, so that they would only elect one Deputy in each. In Dublin, for example, all 13 constituencies were now to be three-seaters, so that on the basis of the voting in the previous election Fianna Fáil could only get 13 seats out of 39. Tully was delighted with his handiwork, and went round Leinster House boasting that never again would Fianna Fáil be able to form a Government.

This kind of prophecy of course is always dangerous, as was shown by the sweeping Fianna Fáil victory in the first election held under the 'Tullymander'. But in the short term everyone did believe Tully – the Coalition parties, the newspapers and their political correspondents, many people even in Fianna Fáil. When therefore Liam Cosgrave went to see the President in May 1977 to ask for a dissolution of the Dáil, he was confident that all would go well for the Coalition in the ensuing General Election.

'Bring Back Jack!'

The result of the 1977 General Election was not alone the most decisive there had ever been (an overall majority of 20), it was also the most surprising. That is, it came as a great surprise to the media: all the newspapers and all the political correspondents were convinced that Fianna Fáil were going to lose. One day towards the end of the campaign, I was in the news room of the *Evening Press*, and the Editor asked me who was going to win. I said – what I *knew* to be true – that Fianna Fáil would get an overall majority, and the whole office burst into laughter.

I suppose it is true to say that political correspondents normally do expect Fianna Fáil to lose elections (wishful thinking?), but in this instance there was the special circumstance of the Tully gerrymander of the constituencies. As a result of this, Fianna Fáil would have lost a large number of seats even without any change in voting patterns.

There were three main reasons for the Fianna Fáil victory. The first was the plain fact that the Cosgrave Coalition was very unpopular. The quadrupling of oil prices in 1973 led to a rapid rise in inflation (up to 18 per cent at one point), unemployment doubled, and there was much resistance to the Government's tax policies. Cosgrave himself was not popular, and there had been a most adverse reaction to his behaviour in connection with the crisis leading to the resignation of President Cearbhall Ó Dálaigh. There had been strong criticism also of his strange decision as Taoiseach to vote against his own Government's Family Planning Bill in July 1974.

The second – and perhaps the most important – reason for the Fianna Fáil election victory was the astonishing popularity of Jack Lynch himself, especially when set against the lack-lustre figure of Liam Cosgrave. The whole campaign revolved round Lynch, with his country-wide tour, the thousands of 'Bring back Jack' tee-shirts, the posters everywhere bearing his name and photograph.

The third factor in the winning of the election was the policy document published at the start of the campaign, and largely drafted by Martin O'Donoghue, a Trinity College Professor who for several years had been economics advisor to Jack Lynch. The 1977 Manifesto promised a large number of new jobs, grants for first-time house purchasers, the abolition of rates on dwelling houses, and the elimination of road tax on small cars. This Manifesto has in later years been singled out as the reason why Fianna Fáil won the election: it was obviously a very important factor, but it was just one of many issues that influenced the voters in this election. Nowadays it is fashionable to describe the 1977 Manifesto as an irresponsible gamble, the origin of all our later financial problems. In fact its immediate results were excellent, with a halving of inflation and a rapid increase in employment. The later difficulties resulted from an unwillingness to change economic policies as world conditions changed.

In the 1977 campaign my task was to run Jack Lynch's tour, in which he covered over forty constituencies in less than three weeks. It was an amazing effort, in which he showed that he still retained much of the stamina that had brought him such fame in his GAA days. I am afraid that from time to time I had to place still further burdens on him.

I would get angry telephone calls from remote parts of the country – angry because directors of election in rural areas tended to assume that Dublin was populated by idiots, none of whom knew how to run an election. The gist of such a telephone call would be that there was a large and important area that Jack was not going to visit. None of our candidates came from there, but there was a strong enemy candidate who was going to clean up all the votes. We were going to lose a seat unless we did something about it. I would point out to the caller that his own constituency director of elections had agreed to Jack's schedule, but this never mollified anyone: I would be treated to unprintable remarks about the director. I knew of course that all this was nonsense, but in the interest of local morale I would do my best to fit Jack in, if at all possible. As a result, I got occasional pained reports from him describing the scene as his cavalcade of cars leapt from pot hole to pot hole at 60 miles an hour along the winding bog roads of the West of Ireland.

Sometimes there were problems that I could not solve. Even Jack Lynch had to stop every now and then to sleep or eat, and this would always be at some traditional Fianna Fáil establishment. The decisions as to where he should stop were of course a delicate matter, that could only be decided at local level. One day I had a frantic telephone call from Gort, Co. Galway. There was a certain restaurant in the town that had always been at the heart of the local organisation: de Valera had eaten there, Lemass had eaten there, and now Lynch was going to drive through the town without stopping there. This was simply inconceivable. I asked a few questions, and it turned out that the town of Gort at that period was split between two separate constituencies. The crowd from the other constituency had highjacked Jack, and he was having his tea with them. All I could do was to tell them they were going to have to settle this question themselves, and I added a mild suggestion that they might remember that in this election they were all supposed to be on the same side. Where did Jack have his tea? I never found out!

In the last week of the campaign it had been arranged that Lynch would come back and spend a few hours in each Dublin constituency. So I telephoned round the dozen or so directors of election and arranged Jack's schedule with them. With Charlie Haughey's constituency of Artane, however, there was a problem. I had a telephone call from him in which he said that they were getting on very well in Artane, and they did not need Lynch. But if I told him that Lynch wanted to go there, then they would let him in.

I had no intention of falling into that trap: the party leader was entitled to visit any constituency he wanted to, the question of seeking permission did not arise. So I told Charlie that Jack didn't care whether he visited Artane or not. But if he went to all the other areas and just missed out one, then this would be seized on by Coalition speakers as a sign of Fianna Fáil disunity. We settled it on that basis, and in due course Lynch arrived in Artane, to be received by Haughey much as the lord of the manor might receive a distinguished guest.

After the votes had been counted Fianna Fáil emerged with 84 seats. Three Coalition Ministers were ousted, one of whom – to universal joy – was Conor Cruise-O'Brien. I was told that at election counts in different parts of the country, the news of his defeat was greeted with applause from all parties, including his own Labour party. He had antagonised nearly everybody by his increasingly anti-national views, and his almost fascist endeavours to control what was said or done on Irish Radio and Television. After the election, he gained a seat in the Seanad but resigned a year later to become editor of the English newspaper the *Observer*. From then on he became 'Britain's favourite Irishman.'

A couple of days after the election I wrote a private letter to the then Editor of *The Irish Times*, the late Fergus Pyle. In it I pointed out that on a number of occasions during the campaign, he had published surveys of the opinions on various subjects of supporters of the different parties. These polls must obviously have been based on a primary question in each case, that is, 'What Party do you support?' Yet his newspaper never published this basic information.

I added in my letter that on the basis of what he did publish I had made my own calculations, which showed clearly that *The Irish Times* polls envisaged support for Fianna Fáil amounting to around 51 per cent to 55 per cent. I found it hard to understand the insistence in the newspaper, day-by-day, even up to the day of the count, that the Coalition Government were certain to win the election. At the same time, their own polls showed that there was about to be a landslide win for Fianna Fáil.

He replied to me in some detail, but the gist of his letter was that they simply did not believe the extent of the swing as shown in their polls. But he did not make any effort to explain why, having had what, at the very least, was a warning that there was a massive swing to Fianna Fáil, he and his political 'experts' continued saying the opposite. It seems to have been a case of 'if you don't like a poll's result, then ignore it.'

I can make one small addition to the story of the 1977 General Election. At that time Ireland had ten members at the European Parliament, nominated by the Dáil and Seanad: five Fianna Fáil, three Fine Gael and two Labour. I went to see Jack Lynch, and pointed out that Fianna Fáil now had the numbers to take six of the seats in the Parliament. Lynch said he would rather leave things as they were; he didn't want to cause any controversy. I suggested that to leave the Opposition with one seat more than they were entitled to would enable them to build up someone as a candidate in the forthcoming Direct Elections to the European Parliament, due in 1979. To this Lynch replied that the Parliament was of no importance anyway, and if we did do badly in the European Elections then we would have three years in which to make up any ground lost, before we would face another General Election. I retreated from this interview in a state of dazed astonishment. In the event, Brian Lenihan and others were able to overrule Lynch, and the Government duly decided that Fianna Fáil would take the extra seat in the Parliament to which they were entitled.

In the new Government George Colley remained on as Minister for Finance. Martin O'Donoghue became Minister for Economic Planning and Development on his first day in the Dáil. His new responsibilities cut across the normal functions of the Department of Finance, and it may be that later on this division of responsibilities hindered the taking of necessary decisions.

All went well for the first couple of years after the election, but in 1979 there came the second oil crisis which led to huge increases in oil prices everywhere. Economic depression was widespread throughout the Western world. As a small island economy without any oil resources of our own, we were particularly affected. I don't know just where the responsibility lay, but neither of our two Economics Ministers seemed to realise that everything had changed. The policy that was correct in 1977, designed to create boom conditions, should have been abandoned at once in the world depression of 1979. For whatever reason, action was not taken, things were left to drift, and as a result the country was for a number of years faced with unnecessarily severe financial problems.

The first Direct Elections to the European Parliament, in 1979, took place at a time of increasing inflation, protest marches against the burden of income tax, prolonged postal and refuse-collection strikes, and a severe petrol shortage that resulted in infuriated motorists having to queue for hours to get 50 pence worth of petrol. In the General Election two years earlier, Fianna Fáil had got over half the total vote: this now fell to just over a third, and the party won only five of the fifteen Irish seats in the Parliament.

This was bad enough, but a few months later in November 1979, there were two by-elections in Cork; both of them were lost. In Jack Lynch's own constituency of Cork City, where his personal vote two years earlier had been over 20,000, the Fine Gael candidate won easily. There had been a complete collapse of the Fianna Fáil vote. Lynch was so shaken by this that within a few days he announced his intention of resigning the leadership of the Party. There was a brief two-day campaign fought between George Colley and Charlie Haughey. Almost all Lynch's Ministers backed Colley, who felt certain of victory, and his defeat (by 44 to 38) came about as a result of a back bench revolt against the failures of Government policy.

After the great election victory of 1977 there had been a period of general euphoria; Jack Lynch was the hero, the future seemed bright. But over the next two years everything changed. Problems of all kinds built up, public opinion was turning against Fianna Fáil, and there was no sense that the Government knew what it was doing. Jack Lynch had had his great moment of victory, but after that he seemed to lose interest. Morale amongst the Deputies declined steadily.

Lynch had said to me that it did not really matter if we did badly in the elections to the European Parliament. What he had not understood was the extent to which such a defeat could create a sense of gloom and depression, not merely amongst the Fianna Fáil Deputies, but in the Organisation as a whole. It was not merely that a large part of Fianna Fáil support in the country had disappeared almost overnight, but that the leadership had no apparent plans for dealing with the situation. I suspect that the extent of this feeling was not understood by Jack Lynch. Certainly Colley, immersed in his Cabinet cocoon, had no idea at all of what back bench Deputies were thinking.

Over a period of some months I listened to Deputies talking about the political situation – their complaints about specific Government policies, about the lack of leadership, about their worries for the future. During this period I never heard anyone suggest that a motion should be put down at the Parliamentary Party calling on Jack to resign. I am perfectly certain that

Haughey knew all about this back bench discontent, and that as an ambitious man he was ready to leap in should Jack Lynch slip. But I doubt if he needed to do much to encourage the discontent; all the elements of a back bench revolt were already there. Lynch's decision to resign, however, was entirely his own, and was in no way forced on him by Party pressure.

George Colley thought that he had been deprived of the leadership by some form of underhand trickery. In fact he lost because he was associated in many Deputies' minds with Government policies that had failed. They felt that he would be another Lynch, but without his charisma: under Colley, they believed, Fianna Fáil would continue to drift aimlessly in a hostile political environment. I know that some Deputies who voted for Charlie Haughey were not at all sure what would happen under his leadership. But they felt that at least something would happen, whereas under Colley it would simply be more of the same. No one of course – no matter what side they voted on in the leadership election – imagined for a moment the financial landmine that 18 years later would destroy the reputation of Charles Haughey. Colley himself laid down certain political conditions, but accepted the office of Tánaiste. He also became Minister for Energy.

Charles Haughey therefore became leader of Fianna Fáil, and was elected Taoiseach by the Dáil on 11 December 1979, but he never had the support of a united Government. From the start, Colley and his group of supporters worked against him, and as the years went by there was an unprecedented series of organised leaks from Cabinet meetings. These went to the media, and even on occasion straight to Opposition parties. The solid party unity that had been such a characteristic of Fianna Fáil had been abandoned.

So far as I myself was concerned, this period was a watershed in my career. Having failed to gain election to the European Parliament in the first Direct Election, I took up a position as Director on the Secretariat of the EEC Council in Brussels, in April 1980, and remained there for six years. Thus my nearly 40 years in active politics came to an end.

Looking Abroad

For the first 20 years or so of my direct involvement in political affairs – during the 1950s and 1960s – it could truthfully be said that we had no foreign policy. We were perhaps unique in Europe in having no Parliamentary Committee for External Affairs. The Dáil did indeed have an annual debate on external affairs, but it was poorly attended and attracted little interest. The success of any Minister for External Affairs was gauged by the number of speeches he managed to make at international assemblies on the perennial subject of Partition. Britain, as the country nearest us and the one with which we conducted almost our entire external trade, was of primary interest to us.

The Continental European countries, in the days before air travel, were geographically remote. We knew little about them, nor did we speak any of their languages. Nor indeed did they know anything about us. This was a period when we tended to be confused with Iceland. I remember travelling across France by train and being asked where I came from. Ireland, I said, upon which there was a long pause. Finally the man sitting opposite me understood: 'Ah!', he said, 'de Valera, Sinn Féin, Bang Bang!' Clearly there was a need for some mutual understanding between Ireland and the rest of Europe. Therein lay the importance – at least for Ireland – of the founding of the Council of Europe in 1949, just four years after the end of the Second World War. We were one of the first ten countries to join, and each year the Dáil and Seanad appointed a total of eight members to attend the sessions of the Council, held in Strasbourg.

The Council has always been associated in particular with the protection of Human Rights. The European Court of Human Rights was set up in 1950, and it also sits in Strasbourg. However, in the early years, the

Council's primary importance lay, perhaps, in the fact that it provided a forum in which the deadly enemies of the War years were able to come together in peace and amity. In this respect it was an initial experiment that pointed the way to the foundation later on of the European Economic Community.

In the earlier years of our membership of the Council of Europe we tended to think of the Assembly in Strasbourg as a useful forum in which we could speak of the evils of Partition: Eamon de Valera himself (then in Opposition) turned up at an early Session as a delegate in order to deliver an oration on this topic. There was, I think, a basic misunderstanding in our attitude. We believed implicitly in the justice of our cause, and thought that once we had explained it to the nations of the world then they would accept and support our stand on Partition.

Long since, we have come to realise that no one wants to hear about the grievances of other countries. Each has enough problems of its own without getting involved in other people's difficulties. I was reminded of this unfortunate fact some 20 years later (in 1975) when George Colley and I were invited to go to Athens to talk to the Greek Management Association about Ireland's experience of the EEC. One of the Greek businessmen came up to me afterwards and asked if I thought that when Greece joined the EEC they would be able to solve the Cyprus problem. I had to tell him that his countrymen would be wise to say nothing at all about Cyprus, as that would be a certain way of damaging Greek prestige in the eyes of their fellow Community members.

In April 1953, I was sent as a delegate to the Council of Europe. This for me was the beginning of a life-long interest in European affairs, though I can't say that I was able to work up much interest in the debates at the Plenary Sessions. The Council was essentially a talking shop, as it still is today. The only excitement was caused by the British delegation, who brought to the Council the full range of somewhat childish inter-party hostilities that was their normal practice in the House of Commons in London. No matter how lacklustre the subject under discussion, the Labour and Tory members would find something on which to disagree, and they would begin shouting at one another, to the obvious amazement of their Continental colleagues. Outside the Assembly they never seemed to socialise, and they stayed in different hotels. In one of the Council restaurants one day, I was talking to Tom Peart, a British Labour delegate who in later years became Minister for Agriculture. After a while a harmless-looking individual came through the door. Peart looked at him and said, 'Huh! You can smell a Tory.'

During the year that I spent at the Council I was a member of the Committee for Population and Refugees. At that period there were still several million war refugees in Central Europe, mainly Germans who had been expelled from East Prussia, Silesia, the Sudetenland and other areas. The Committee carried out an extensive tour of refugee camps in various parts of Germany, and we interviewed a series of rather sad camp committees – always sitting under wall-maps still including their ancestral homelands as part of Germany.

While sympathising with their plight, I hoped that those wall-maps did not represent a future intention to take back their ancient lands by force. As things turned out, of course, there was no need to worry about such a possibility. In time, the millions of destitute refugees were successfully absorbed into the general population, and no one any longer queries the post-war boundaries of Germany.

During this tour of refugee camps we arrived one Sunday evening in Cologne. I took a walk through the centre of the City (the streets round the Cathedral and the main railway station), where an area perhaps two miles square was filled with milling crowds looking at the brightly lit shop windows. It was perhaps half-an-hour before I happened to look upwards towards the sky, to find to my shocked amazement that not a single building in that whole area was more than ten feet high. The entire centre of Cologne had been destroyed during the War, and these single-story buildings had been erected as a temporary measure. I realised of course that Cologne was not unique, that all the great cities of Germany had suffered at least as much damage, but this was the first time that I had actually seen for myself what war can do.

It was in 1953 also that I was asked to become a founder member of the Irish branch of the European Movement. I was not sure what I should do about this. Sections of the Movement on the Continent were known to back a sort of United States of Europe, in which the European States would be required to give up their sovereignty to a central Government, on the American model. Obviously no such proposal would be acceptable in Ireland.

I raised the matter therefore at the next meeting of the Fianna Fáil National Executive. I explained the situation, upon which de Valera said he thought that I should accept the invitation to join the European Movement, so that I could keep the Executive informed as to what was going on. So I joined the Movement as a spy! But in fact my services as a spy were not needed: from the start the European Movement in Ireland performed a valuable service in keeping us all informed about developments. It played a big part later on in the EEC Referendum campaign, and at the present day is active in publicising and explaining European Union policies.

In 1953 our Council of Europe delegation had spent a leisurely three days driving in three Garda squad cars from Dublin to Strasbourg – and another three days coming back. All this had changed by the year 1970 when – as Cathaoirleach of the Seanad – I led a delegation of Deputies and Senators to the Annual Conference of the Inter-Parliamentary Union at The Hague. A simple air flight had replaced what in earlier years would have been a two-day journey.

I am afraid I have no memory at all of what took place during the meetings of this Conference; the Inter-Parliamentary Union is like that, nothing very much ever happens. One day, however, an invitation arrived for a Reception at the Soviet Embassy. I gathered that such an invitation was received at all these annual conferences – intended for leaders of delegations only. I duly accepted and turned up at the Embassy, not realising that in doing so I was creating something of a sensation. It seemed that I was the first Irishman who had ever accepted the Soviet invitation. Our delegations to the Conference were always led by either the Ceann Comhairle or the Cathaoirleach, and in the past none of these had cared to risk the disasters that might befall them should they enter the portals of the Soviet Embassy.

In fact no sooner had I arrived than I myself faced something of a disaster. I was greeted with enthusiasm in the entrance hall by a large lady of commanding appearance, who thrust a glass of vodka into my hand. I declined the offer, explaining that I did not drink (which was true). However, it seemed that non-drinkers did not exist in Soviet society. 'But this is vodka,' she explained severely. The atmosphere had changed. It now seemed that I had turned up at the Soviet Embassy only to insult them.

For the sake of my country, therefore, I took the glass of vodka and slugged it down in her presence, to show that I really was accepting the Soviet Union's hospitality. I then rapidly retreated round a corner before she could insist that I take another one. During the Reception I came across a man with perfect English who turned out to be an official interpreter, one of those who travelled everywhere with such Soviet dignitaries as Brezhnev and Khruschev. He told me how happy they all were that I had accepted their invitation. 'You are a very small country and we are a very large one,' he said, 'but, you know, we feel these things.' I thought to myself how strange it was that here we had a country which went out of its way to antagonise everyone, and yet was so anxious to be liked.

A few months later, as Cathaoirleach, I led another delegation, this time to France. There were just six of us, myself and five Deputies, in what was described as a 'Groupe d'Amitié' (Friendship Group), returning a similar visit to Ireland paid by French Parliamentarians. We spent a week in France, engaged for most of the time in what might be described as tourism, interspersed with numerous polite speeches.

Here again we had a little problem with alcohol. Just one of our number drank wine in moderation, but none of the rest of us drank alcohol at all. I had to explain this phenomenon to our hosts, who must have found it surprising, but were willing – unlike the Soviets – to accept that such eccentrics may indeed exist. So wherever we went, even in the little Town Hall in some remote rural area, we would find a half dozen bottles of Evian water along the table. Just one of our five non-drinkers, the late Flor Crowley from Cork, preferred to drink coke, and asked for this wherever we went.

At one stage on our tour we visited the town of Vichy, and were brought to the Casino, at which Flor won £150. Next day we were driven some 60 miles to Roanne, where we were to have dinner at a celebrated restaurant called 'Les Frères Troisgros'. As we drove along in the bus, Flor Crowley was approached by the French official who accompanied us everywhere. He explained to Flor that we were going to one of the great restaurants of France, one of only 12 that had been awarded three 'Michelin' stars. He went on into further rhapsodies about this restaurant, and ended up saying, 'Mr Crowley, please Mr Crowley, do not ask for coke.'

Early on in this tour we were in Paris, and our schedule one morning listed an 'entretien' at 11 a.m. with the Foreign Affairs Committee of the Chamber of Deputies. I asked at our Embassy what was involved – an 'entretien', amongst other things, means 'a conversation or talk'. No one knew anything about it, but it was assumed that we were probably going to be given a cup of coffee. So off we went, and we were ushered in to a large room with a couple of dozen people already sitting there. We were led to our own seats, after which we were greeted by a man who was obviously presiding. Then he looked at me and said 'Now, Monsieur le Président, would you tell us what problems Ireland is likely to face in joining the European Economic Community?'

This was quite one of the worst moments of my life. Here I was, without any briefing, suddenly plunged into what became a two-hour cross-examination by this most prestigious committee. It was not even as if I (or the other members of our Group) had much detailed knowledge about the EEC. This was a couple of years before we joined, and negotiations for our entry were still at an early stage. However there was nothing to be done, except to look confident and give the impression that I knew what I was talking about.

The one thing that saved me was that each question was asked in French and then interpreted into English, so I at least had a few seconds in which to consider my reply. After about an hour I was able to turn over some of the questions to other members of the Group, particularly Dick Burke and Jim Tully (both of them former Ministers). I think in the end we did all right, but if so, there were no thanks due to our Paris Embassy.

The President of the Foreign Affairs Committee was a nobleman of ancient lineage called Le Prince de Broglie. A few days later we spent a night at his 500 year old chateau in Normandy where, after dinner, he showed us some of the treasures that had come down through the family over the centuries. I remember two items in particular. He opened a drawer and took out a letter written by St Francis Xavier and then, a couple of minutes later, he produced a sheet of paper with a series of figures written on it. This was the Budget of France for some year in the 17th century, written by the great 'Sun-King' Louis XIV. There were sums listed for the Army, for propaganda, for Court expenses, for the building of the Palace of Versailles. At the end a line was drawn, total expenditure was given, and below this the King's own signature. Life was simpler in those days.

Some years later the Prince de Broglie was shot down on a street in Paris. I asked how this could possibly have happened and was told that the murderers were unknown, but that it was suspected that the Prince had for several years been involved with some unsavoury underworld characters. It was thought he may have owed them money. What about his distinguished position as President of the Foreign Affairs Committee? I was told that while no one knew anything for certain about his activities, the Prince had, over a period, been quietly eased out of this and any other positions he held in the Gaullist Party.

This meeting in Paris was a portent for the future. Our isolation as an island in the Atlantic set on the western fringe of Europe, was coming to an end. Until the early 1970s Irish politicians had kept in occasional touch with other countries at annual Conferences, or at the regular sessions of the Council of Europe. Now we were all faced with a new prospect – that of 'joining Europe'. That very phrase, of course, 'joining Europe', was a reflection of our long-term sense of isolation: our immediate world consisted of Ireland and Britain. 'Europe' was a long way away.

In January 1972, we signed the Treaty of Accession to the EEC, after which for the first time we had to consider seriously our future as a 'European' country. Before we could 'join Europe' we had to amend the Constitution by Referendum, so a long campaign began in which the arguments for and against entry to the EEC were marshalled. Some of the arguments for entry were obvious. Our farmers were bound to gain, as under the Common Agricultural Policy they could for the first time look forward to getting an economic price for their produce. It was clear as well that if Britain joined and we did not, then there would be trading and other barriers between us, and also between the Republic and Northern Ireland. There were other arguments also in favour of entry, but these were the ones that were of particular interest to the general public.

I think it would be fair to say that the main worry that many people had with respect to the EEC was the inevitable loss of sovereignty that was involved. Had we spent all those centuries trying to assert our national identity, to have it submerged in a Europe of which we were only a tiny part? In the event 83 per cent voted in favour of entry in the Referendum, and we formally became one of the EEC member States on 1 January 1973.

Just a few months earlier, I was at a Dinner given by Dr Patrick Hillery, then Minister for Foreign Affairs. The Guest of Honour was Gaston Thorn, the Minister for Foreign Affairs of Luxembourg, who made a speech that impressed me greatly at the time, and that I have never forgotten. He told us that he quite understood that as a small country of only 3 million people, we might be worried that we would be swallowed up in a Community that had a total population of more than 300 million. He wanted therefore to tell us something about his own country, the Grand Duchy of Luxembourg, which had a population of only one-tenth of ours. 'I can tell you,' he said, 'that in the 15 years since we joined the EEC, our country has had more influence in the world than at any time in its previous thousand years of history.' I may add that my wife, Gráinne, who was seated next to Gaston Thorn at the dinner, kept him well informed about Irish worries: she has always had her doubts about the future of Irish sovereignty in the European Union.

In October, 1972, the Seanad received an invitation to send a delegation to the European Parliament. We duly turned up in Strasbourg, and we spent a busy few days there being informed about the functions and procedures of the Parliament, and about the policies of the various Political Groups. So far as I personally was concerned, I was totally fascinated by the whole Parliamentary apparatus – the process of European legislation, the working of the Committee system and the Political Groups with members from many different countries.

By the time our Seanad delegation came back to Dublin I had decided that I wanted to become a member of the European Parliament. At that time the members of the Parliament were nominated by the national Parliaments, so I went to see Jack Lynch and told him that I would like to resign my position as Cathaoirleach, in order to become a member. In due course I was informed that the Government had decided that I should be nominated as one of the five Fianna Fáil members.

It was made clear to me, however, that as a Senator I could not be the leader of the group. This last message was less than helpful. I had no ambition to be leader, and I was perfectly willing to go along with the theory that the heavens would fall were a mere Senator to start dictating to a Dáil Deputy. But what was the point of telling one person he could not be leader, and then not appointing anyone else to do the job? In any event where, as in this instance, only five people were involved, the question of 'leadership' simply did not arise. If a decision had to be taken, then it would emerge during an informal discussion over a cup of coffee. Admittedly someone might have to suggest that a decision needed to be taken, and perhaps arrange a time and place for taking it, but that is more a task for a secretary than for a leader. From the first I took on this type of co-ordinating work, simply because no one else seemed to want to do it.

On a more formal basis, however, I found myself enmeshed in Continental concepts of protocol. The President of the French Senate is, in terms of protocol, the second most important person in the country: he becomes President of the Republic should the holder of that office die or become incapacitated. As Cathaoirleach of the Seanad I once visited Alain Poher, the President of the French Senate. He lived in a beautiful Palace in central Paris, surrounded by well-kept gardens. Everywhere one looked there were marble halls, pillars, grand staircases and tapestries. When the President went in to preside at the Senate he was accompanied by men in medieval armour. When I came back to Dublin our Seanad somehow did not seem quite the same. As usual, I had trouble finding a space to park my car.

As a former Cathaoirleach, therefore, I was often treated abroad with an exaggerated respect way beyond my actual status back in Ireland. From the first day of our arrival at the Parliament, I was addressed by all and sundry as 'Monsieur le Président'. I was made a temporary member of the Bureau (Parliament's governing body), and I was asked to make the opening speech on behalf of the Irish delegation at the first Session of the Parliament held after Denmark, Ireland and the United Kingdom had joined the EEC.

European Parliament

Ireland joined the European Economic Community on 1 January, 1973. Later in that month the Irish members set off for Strasbourg, to attend our first session of the European Parliament. There were ten of us, three Senators and seven Deputies: for all of us a quite new phase in our political careers had started.

So far as I was concerned, while I still took a very active part in the proceedings of the Seanad in Dublin, my primary involvement for the next seven years was in European politics. The Parliament in full session met (at that period) alternately in Strasbourg or in Luxembourg. Its Committees and Political Groups normally met in Brussels, but meetings also took place from time to time all over the nine Member States of the EEC. Every week I had to take at least one flight to the Continent and back; there were endless nights spent in hotels. It was the most exhausting period of my life, but also the most fascinating.

My first task at the European Parliament was to draft and deliver the opening speech on behalf of all the Irish Members at the Ceremonial Sitting held in Strasbourg on 16 January 1973. In this speech, couched in the somewhat formal terms customary on such occasions, I spoke of the reasons that had impelled Ireland to join the Community and of what we hoped to achieve as Members of the European Parliament. It may be of interest to give the speech here, as a reminder of our vision of the EEC on our entry some 25 years ago.

> *Mr President,*
> *This is a great and moving occasion for those of us who have come from Ireland to join from today in the deliberations of*

this European Parliament. In the first place, it is for us a tangible sign of the membership of our country in the European Economic Community. Our presence at this meeting today is a reflection of the decision made by our people last year, when after a long and strongly argued debate, they voted by an overwhelming majority of 83 per cent to join the EEC.

For us in Ireland it is not really a question, as the phrase goes, of our 'going into Europe'. Although we are a small island situated on the very fringe of Europe, we have, all through our long history, thought of ourselves as Europeans. Our scholars, our saints, brought civilisation and culture to many parts of the Continent, our soldiers fought in the armies of France and Spain. The traces of the Irish are to be seen to this day in many parts of the Continent – in the names of places and of families and in the ancient libraries and monasteries that our ancestors left behind them. Our interest in Europe is in fact nothing new. For many centuries we in Ireland have felt the closest ties of friendship and affection for the countries of the Continent of Europe.

We have, therefore, Mr President, a profound admiration for the inspiration that prompted the founders of the EEC, at a time when much of Europe was still devastated by war, to determine that the nations of Europe would never again engage in such a conflict.

We welcome, and we are happy to play our part in realising, the ideals set out so clearly in the Preamble to the Treaty of Rome. We join in the pledge there given by the Six of their determination 'to lay the foundations of an ever closer union among the peoples of Europe' and in their affirmation also that the essential objective of their efforts would be 'the constant improvement of the living and working conditions of their peoples.'

We have followed with admiration the progress that has been made during the past 15 years towards the achievement of these aims. In particular the traditional gap in living standards between those who live in cities and those who work on the land is being steadily narrowed as a result of the beneficial operations of the Common Agricultural Policy.

A beginning, though as yet only a beginning, has been made in the even more difficult and more important task of ending the great disparities that exist between the social and economic development of the different regions of Western Europe. There also remains the task of fulfilling our common obligations as members of the Community to help in the economic and social progress of the developing countries. When the final history of our European Economic Community comes some day to be written, the ultimate success of the Community will be judged not on the extent to which it has succeeded in making the rich richer but on the extent to which it has brought a new hope, a new and a higher quality of life, to those who live in the poorer regions of Europe and of the underdeveloped countries overseas.

While recognising, therefore, that much still remains to be done in the carrying out of the ideals set before us in the Treaty of Rome, we rejoice that so much real progress has in fact been made in setting up the institutions of the new Europe. We are fortunate to be joining the European Economic Community just at the moment when the early gains have been consolidated, and at a time when the great leap forward envisaged in the Paris Summit is about to get under way. We look forward, those of us who come from Ireland, to playing our part in the long and arduous programme of work that has been promised for the coming years.

In a more direct and personal way, this meeting marks for us who come here for the first time today the beginning of our task as members of the European Parliament. However much we may recognise its existing deficiencies, the European Parliament remains for us, as for all peoples of the enlarged Community, the essential democratic framework without which the whole concept of European integration would be rendered futile. We look forward, therefore, all of us, to the varied tasks which await us here, just as we look forward to the prospect of joining with our European colleagues in the

> *activities of the Political Groups. We will do all we can to co-operate in the struggle to increase the powers and the prestige of this Parliament so that it may become a fully equal partner with the other Community institutions.*
>
> *I thank you, Mr President, for your kind words of welcome, and I can give you the assurance of our intense and active interest in the proceedings of this great European Parliament.*

Once the polite speech-making of the first day was over, the ordinary work of the Parliament resumed. In particular, for our Fianna Fáil members, there began the search for a suitable Political Group that we could join. This was an important matter, since under the procedures of the Parliament, Independent members have few rights, and are greatly restricted in their political activities. The three Fine Gael members had long-standing connections with the Christian Democrats and the two Labour members of course joined the Socialist Group in the Parliament; but we in Fianna Fáil had no such obvious grouping that we could join. There were at that time six Groups in the Parliament, of which two could be ignored – the British Conservatives and the Communists. We had little difficulty in deciding against joining the Christian Democrats: their Fine Gael members would have had to agree to our joining, a situation that could hardly be acceptable to Fianna Fáil.

In any event we disliked the strong confessional element in sections of the Christian Democrat movement, which we felt was in conflict with the non-sectarian traditions of Irish republicanism. Before we had even joined the EEC, the Christian Democrat Group sent to Dublin their senior Vice President, Signor Bersani, to try to persuade Fianna Fáil to join them. I had a cup of tea with him in the Dáil Restaurant, and he went on at some length about the virtues of his Group. After a while I decided to try an experiment. I pointed to Deputy Ben Briscoe, who was sitting nearby, and explained that he was a Jew. Suppose, I asked Bersani, that Ben was a member of our delegation to the Parliament; would he be eligible to be a member of the Christian Democrat Group? No, said Bersani, he would not. That seemed to settle the matter. Ben Briscoe had in fact no intention at that time of going to the Parliament, but we could hardly consider joining a Political Group that would refuse to accept a Jewish member.

As regards the Socialist Group, we felt that we would have many points in common with them, but we could not accept their views on agricultural policy. Over the years at Strasbourg they had campaigned for lower food prices for urban workers, paying no attention to the effect that this would have in reducing the living standards of small farmers. In any event, to become members of this Group we would have to become members of the Socialist International, and gain the agreement of the two Irish members, Conor Cruise-O'Brien and Justin Keating.

As a result of our investigations at the Parliament, it became clear to us that there were only two Political Groups that we might consider joining. One of these, called 'Liberal and Allied Parties', was a loose-knit and very varied Group, with 25 members deriving from 13 national Parties, spread over eight Member States. No single Party represented in it had more than three members.

I myself was in favour of our joining the Liberal Group. Its loose internal discipline and absence of any serious policies of its own would, I felt, give us every opportunity to assert our own individuality and to push our own policies. As the largest single Party in the Group, Fianna Fáil would be bound to have a considerable influence on its activities. We would in effect retain many of the advantages of independence. while obtaining the benefits to be had from membership of a Political Group.

The other Group in which we were interested was the European Democratic Union (EDU), whose 19 members were all representatives of the French Gaullist Party. We had extended talks with the President and other leading members of this Group, and we were all impressed with their candour and clear thinking.

On the question of our joining this Group, however, there was a division in our ranks. Three favoured joining the EDU, one was uncommitted, and I was against. The three in favour felt that the Gaullist Group had a strong rural and agricultural bias, a respect for traditional values, a desire to defend the concept of the family farm and, in general, an outlook very close to that of the Irish people as a whole. It was felt also that this Group accepted the basic principles of the EEC but did not believe in progressing too fast towards a federal Europe. It stressed the importance of preserving the national character of each of the countries of the EEC, and of the authority of national Governments. This should be our aim also.

On the other hand, I felt that it would be a mistake to join the EDU, which was looked upon as a purely French Group, interested only in propagating the policies of the Gaullist Government in Paris. We would face hostility in the media on the grounds that we were adopting an anti-European stance at the Parliament. In addition, I felt, as just five Irishmen amongst some twenty Frenchmen, we would have very little scope for asserting our own policies.

I set out all these arguments in a memorandum that I sent to Jack Lynch. About five months went by, until finally the decision came that we were to join the Gaullist Group. So on 22 June 1973, Brian Lenihan, Michael O'Kennedy and myself turned up in Paris. We rapidly settled matters with our new French colleagues. The old European Democratic Union was dissolved and replaced by the Irish-French European Progressive Democrat Group (EPD).

It may be asked why we chose such a meaningless title for our new Group? As so often with the European Parliament, language problems had arisen. I had discussed this question with the Gaullists at the most recent session of the Parliament; each time I suggested a possible title (in English), they said this would not translate adequately into French – and vice versa. So we decided on the EPD title. At least this would proclaim that we were European, Progressive and Democratic: what more could one want?

Once everything had been decided in Paris, before signing anything we had to ring up Jack Lynch in Dublin to get his formal agreement. There was a little problem, we were told; there was a telephonic delay of 2 hours. This was the period when our own telephone service was at its worst, so I found it somehow encouraging to find that the French service was just as bad. Never mind, our new colleagues said, we can use the telephone in the office of the Minister for Defence. We were brought in to the palatial quarters of the Minister, and to a very large desk on which there was an elegant instrument looking as if it was made of gold. I assumed that this object would get us through to Dublin within seconds, but no, there was still a delay of one hour. So we waited, finally got through to Jack Lynch, received his blessing and signed the document that brought our new Group into being.

Although I had initially opposed our going in with the Gaullists, I never at any time regretted our having made this alliance. I was correct in one thing. As I had prophesied, the media reaction was hostile from the first, and continued to be so. Sometimes this hostility went beyond what was acceptable, such as the occasion when the EPD Group met in Ireland, and Jacques Chirac flew into Cork to take part in our meetings. He was then the Mayor of the City of Paris – in more recent times President of France. On his arrival he gave a press conference, and must have been astonished to be harangued by some of the political correspondents as if he were taking part in a bad-tempered election debate. In the end I had to intervene to put an end to the proceedings.

On the other hand, I was quite wrong in the view I had held that, as five Irishmen amongst twenty French Gaullists, we would have difficulty in asserting our own policies. I believe that in later years there were some occasions when difficulties arose within the Group: but this was never my experience during the years I was at the Parliament. It was inevitable that on occasion there would be some French proposal that could cause us political problems. But the moment they understood that we had a difficulty the matter would be dropped.

We soon learned that at the European Parliament the various nationalities each had their own priorities, and that if we were to have any influence we must take an interest in other people's problems in addition to our own. In our Group, for example, the French had little interest in the Regional policy, but were happy to back any initiative that we took in that field. They, on the other hand, had a passionate interest in matters of which we had previously known nothing, such as those that excited one of our colleagues from the Ardèche, in the South of France. This was a large, solid man called Liogier, who was a member of the Agricultural Committee, and tended to fall asleep during its proceedings. But then someone would mention the word 'peach', upon which he would shoot up in his chair and make an impassioned speech about the rights of peach-growers. It seemed that every now and then in his constituency there would be a glut and the local farmers would dump a lorry-load of peaches on his front door-step, saying 'Now, Monsieur le Député, tell us how we can sell these?' Any mention of olives had the same effect on him.

Inevitably some of the debates at meetings of the Group did not at first make much sense so far as we Irish were concerned. Thus the French kept on having animated discussions about 'le problème de la population.' With the high emigration and unemployment of the early 1970s we knew all about the 'population problem'. But the remedies discussed by our colleagues seemed to make no sense, till we realised that while our problem was that large numbers of young people were coming onto the labour market with no hope of getting work, their problem was that the population was falling due to France's very low birth-rate. Another popular topic for discussion was 'le recyclage des femmes'. I couldn't see why anyone would want to recycle women, until I understood that the expression referred to the retraining of women who had raised their families and wished to come back onto the labour market.

Another thing we had to learn was that our Irish sense of humour was not always understood by the French. One day we were talking to Gérard Bokanowski, who was General Secretary of our Group, when someone mentioned that the island of Guadeloupe in the Caribbean was not a colony but an integral part of France. One of those listening was the late Jim Gibbons (our agricultural expert and one of the few people who understood the Common Agricultural Policy). 'Oh,' he said with deadpan humour, 'then we could hold a Group meeting in Guadeloupe.' We sniggered a bit at this joke, but Bokanowski took it as a serious suggestion. About a year later he came along in triumph to say that we could indeed meet in Guadeloupe: using charter flights, such a meeting need cost no more than one held in southern Italy or some other sunny part of the Continental EEC.

In due course the Group did meet in Guadeloupe, having persuaded the Bureau of Parliament that no extravagance was involved. At this meeting, incidentally, Des O'Malley (still at that time a Fianna Fáil Deputy) had been invited to join in the discussions. Gráinne and I were watching him one day heading far out to sea on some form of one-man beach sail-boat. In an exercise in 'black' humour I said to Gráinne that I hoped he would not drown, as we would lose the resultant by-election. He did in fact have to be rescued and Gráinne told him about my comment. Dessie laughed, and said that I was quite right.

Shortly after we had formed the EPD Group, we were joined by a Danish member. Under the Parliament's rules, a Group received an increase in revenue for each additional nationality included in its membership, so we welcomed Mr Nyborg, even though the policies he espoused were eccentric, to say the least of it. He was in fact a member of the Progress Party of Mogens Glistrup, which proposed to abolish all taxes. It was not clear how the Danish State was supposed to carry on without any tax revenue, but it was said that the Progress Party's defence policy involved the purchase of a tape recorder linked by direct line to the Kremlin. In the event of an outbreak of war, the tape recorder would say, 'We surrender' in Russian. Fortunately Mr Nyborg never raised such issues at the Group: he was too busy arranging to maximise his Parliamentary expenses.

The Danish 'No Tax' Party has languished somewhat since that day. Its leader, Mogens Glistrup, never paid income tax himself, having found, he claimed, a legal way of not doing so. His system was so complex that it took the tax-gatherers several years to work it out, but they got him in the end and sent him off to prison for two years. While he was there his Party replaced him as leader, and ever since he has been trying without success to regain control.

In September 1973, we greeted a more important new member, Brian Lenihan. He had lost his Dáil seat in an exercise in 'vote management' that went wrong; he then gained a Seanad seat, and was nominated a Member of the Parliament. As soon as I heard that this was happening I wrote to Jack Lynch urging him to make Brian Lenihan leader of our Fianna Fáil delegation, and this was done. He remained with us until he recovered his Dáil seat and Cabinet position at the 1977 General Election.

After we had been a while at the European Parliament we realised that, although the various Political Groups each claimed to have their own distinctive policies, in fact there was little scope for the discussion of matters of principle. There was on occasion a certain Left-Right tension, but most of the work of the Parliament was highly technical, so that Party political attitudes did not arise. In Ireland, a great deal of law-making is done by delegated legislation. Were the Dáil and Seanad to agree to a Bill dealing, for example, with safety standards for farm tractors, such a Bill would be quite short. It would provide that all the details should be laid down by Ministerial Order.

In the EEC (now the European Union) there is no such thing as a Ministerial Order, so that there are endless technical debates at Committee level. Thus when the Parliament dealt with the proposals on farm tractors there were detailed discussions about the size of headlights for running on public roads, about the exact design of roll bars to protect the driver in the event of the tractor overturning, on the amount of noise that is permissible, and so on. As always in such cases a detailed Report was agreed at Committee and sent for decision at a Plenary Session of the Parliament. Clearly there was no scope here for differences of principle between Groups.

There will often be much competition for positions as 'Rapporteur', the person who will draft the Report and pilot it through the Committee and then defend it at the Plenary Session. In the case of the tractors there would be no great interest, but with a more prestigious Report there would first of all be a struggle to decide which Group should get it, followed by a war to the knife inside the Group amongst those members anxious to be Rapporteur.

It is in respect of such matters as these that the real rivalry between the Groups is seen. The greatest excitement, of course, is created on the occasions when the numerous Officers of Parliament are up for election. The most important by far is the President of Parliament, but there are also the Vice-Presidents of Parliament and the President of each of the dozen or so Committees. Each Committee will also have a first, second and third Vice-President – there are some who would kill in order to become third Vice-President of some unimportant Committee. Not to be forgotten either are the Presidents, etc., of the various Parliamentary delegations.

All this might suggest that utter chaos reigns on the day of these elections: but in fact almost everything is arranged beforehand by agreement between the Political Groups. The whole thing is a bit like Verdi's opera 'Il Trovatore', where the curtain goes up on Act I and a baritone comes out on the stage and spends ten minutes telling the audience everything that has already happened. Only the President and Vice-

Presidents of Parliament are actually voted upon (though in more recent times the two biggest Groups have agreed to share the Presidency between them, turn and turn about).

I myself was involved on two occasions in the Presidential election. In 1973 the French Gaullists had made an arrangement under which they voted for the Liberal Group's candidate for President, in return for their support next time round. At the next election in 1975 therefore, our EPD Group was entitled to Liberal support for its Presidential candidate. The French members of our Group felt (probably correctly) that there would be a hostile reaction to the prospect of a Gaullist President, so they asked me to stand as the candidate of the Group. I agreed and set off to look for support outside the ranks of the two Groups that were committed to supporting me.

The most promising source of support seemed to be some of the individual British Conservative members, who had no candidate of their own, and might welcome the thought of an English-speaking President. Peter Kirk, the President of their Group, had decreed that their votes should go to the Christian Democrats, but I was able to seduce several of his flock. However just two days before the election he sent back four of his members to London – two of whom were certain votes for me – and in the event I lost the Presidency by just one vote. However, I did become one of a number of Vice-Presidents, and so became involved in the administration of the Parliament as a member of the Bureau.

The next Presidential election was in 1977, and neither the Group nor myself had the slightest intention of getting involved in it. Six months earlier the Italian Chamber of Deputies had appointed a former Prime Minister, Emilio Colombo, to be a member of the European Parliament. The purpose of this appointment was that the Christian Democrats would run him for President, and they expected that in view of his eminence he would be elected by acclamation, without any need for a vote.

Just one hour before the election was due to begin, our Group was visited by a delegation from the Socialist Group, led by the outgoing President of Parliament Georges Spénale. They had been counting heads, and had belatedly come to realise that their candidate could not win the election. They therefore asked me to stand. If I did, they said, they would run their man for the first two rounds, and then swing their votes behind me. It seemed to me that if I was asked to stand by the biggest Group in the Parliament I might as well have a go, so I agreed to their proposal. We therefore sent word round to all the other Groups that we were intending to run a candidate.

Within ten minutes we had a further visit, this time from a very senior member of the Christian Democrat Group. Brian Lenihan went outside from our meeting to talk to him, and came back some time later looking quite shaken. The man's first words to him had been 'How much?' In other words, what did we want in return for withdrawing from the election? One could have understood an offer of the Presidency of a Committee, or some other political titbit of the kind, but the implication that money might be available seemed extraordinary. The emissary from the Christian Democrats spoke English quite well, so I don't think there was any question of a misunderstanding.

It was by now far too late for any canvassing for votes, and in the first two rounds I got just the 19 votes of our Group. At this stage Ludwig Fellermaier, President of the Socialist Group, addressed the Parliament, the first time that such a thing had been done during voting for the Presidency. He said that 'Senator Yeats has proved himself to be a great European and Parliamentarian. We believe he will make a great President.' He went on to pledge his Group's support for me in the final round of voting. In the event, about a dozen left-wing members apparently felt unable to vote for a candidate who was not of the left. Their abstention resulted in the election of a President who was at the extreme right of the Conservative Christian Democrat Group. Colombo won by 85 votes to 77. He never forgave me for running against him, and our relations were cool during all his term of office. In fact I was to have a good deal to do with him, as later on that day I was re-elected Vice-President of Parliament, with 128 out of the 140 votes cast in the election.

The European Parliament can only be understood if one realises that it is unique in having neither Government nor Opposition. The real law-making body is the Council, which attends the Parliament on one day each session, but which is not answerable to the members. All the Groups are united in one thing: the nature of their arguments may vary, but they all attack the Council for its acts, or for its inaction. The nearest thing to a

Government is the European Commission, which is responsible to Parliament. But the Commission has no legislative powers – it drafts the laws, but cannot enact them.

It is not merely with respect to the offices held by members of Parliament that the Political Groups take an interest. Quite unlike the position here in Ireland, everyone on the Continent seems to know the political outlook of the higher officials, and they are selected on this basis. The first time I came to realise this was when, a few months after the formation of our Group, I was asked by its President, Yvon Bourges, to take his place at a meeting of the Bureau of the Parliament. The main business of the meeting, he said, would be the appointment of a half dozen senior officials, all with the rank of Director. My instructions were to insist, on behalf of the Group, that no one should be appointed who had not come first in the competition. This eminently reasonable stance (I thought) was countered by a violent speech by Francis Vals, then President of the Socialist Group. It seemed that none of the successful candidates belonged to the Left, and Vals warned us all that the day would come when the Socialists would have a majority in Parliament. 'Then' he said, 'things will be different.'

There were other respects in which I came to see that the Parliament's officials differed considerably from those we have in Ireland. For most of my time at the Parliament I was a Vice-President, and therefore I was called upon from time to time to preside over the Plenary Sessions. Since I had had several year's experience as Cathaoirleach this presented no difficulty, but the officials sitting on the dais beside me kept on offering what I thought was rather curious advice. So I turned to one of them during a lull in a session and asked: 'Would I be right in thinking that your attitude is that the Rules of Procedure need be followed only when it is convenient?' He looked at me with surprise. 'But of course,' he said. From then on I listened to no further advice, but followed the Rules of Procedure as if I were at home.

While I was at the Parliament there were six working languages (nowadays there are eleven), and I found that the only real problem to be faced in presiding over the Plenary Session was the likelihood that whatever member I was talking to would not understand English. It was no use remonstrating with anyone until – by gestures if necessary – he or she had been persuaded to put on the headphones in order to hear the interpretation of what I was saying.

In general the Parliament was a quiet, well-behaved place, and I only remember two serious rows while I was presiding. The first was an explosion from an Italian Communist member called Squarcialuppi. She erupted in fury because, she claimed, some statement by a French Communist speaker had been attributed to her. This might seem a strange complaint, until one considered the nature of the Communist Group at the Parliament. Almost all its members were from France or Italy: the Italian Communists (at least as we observed them at the Parliament) were no more than slightly left of centre, the French Communists, on the other hand, were way to the left of the Kremlin. So far as I know the Communists at the Parliament never met as a single Group. They had nothing in common except their name. In any event there was nothing I could do with Madame Squarcialuppi except to wait for her to simmer down.

The second row I had to deal with was really nothing to do with me. The officials came to me one day at lunch-time and told me that they faced a problem. Signor Bersani – the man I had met some years earlier in Dublin – had been presiding that morning and had made some rulings that would expose the Presidency to serious challenge. Could I take over the Chair when the Session resumed, and try to sort things out? So during the lunch break I studied the typescript report of the morning session and tried to work out just what had happened.

Bersani had indeed become embroiled in a procedural wrangle with John Prescott, an English member of the Socialist Group (he is now Deputy Prime Minister in the Blair Government). With just a few ill-chosen words, he had infuriated Prescott and reduced the proceedings to near chaos. As I discovered when the session resumed, Prescott was a tough customer to deal with, and it took me some 40 minutes to wear him down. Since I could not admit that a fellow Vice-President could make a mess of things, I had to maintain that where Bersani might seem to have said one thing, he had really said something quite different. I remember at one stage pointing to a comma in the transcript and claiming that this changed the whole meaning of the sentence. I can't say that the Presidency covered itself in glory over the whole thing, but at least by the time we had finished there was no Bersani ruling left that could cause anyone embarrassment.

This whole affair was a good example of a basic difference between the Continental practice and the custom in Britain or Ireland. Once a ruling has been made from the Chair in the Dáil or Seanad that is the end of it; anyone who queries it is in real trouble. At the European Parliament such a ruling is almost an invitation to a debate. The Chairman can be called upon to give a full explanation and justification of his ruling: all and sundry can leap up with points of order, so that whatever topic is supposed to be under discussion may disappear in a procedural maze. Of course, as I have suggested earlier, points of order are not always concerned with what is legally correct – a member may simply not like a ruling.

However, the one constant factor that differentiates the European Parliament from all others is the language problem. At all levels, from the Plenary Session down to the smallest Working Group, no meetings can take place without the presence of the interpreters. Before we even came to the Parliament I had an example of their efficiency. They got in touch with us at the Seanad and asked to be sent some of the cassettes on which our debates were recorded, so that they could get used to the sound of the Irish accents.

No matter how efficient the interpreters may be, debates in the Parliament inevitably lack spontaneity. It is unsafe to make a joke, as by the time a joke made in English reaches the Danes, for example, the speaker may have gone on to some more serious topic and at that stage laughter could be disconcerting. Or the interpreter might not understand the joke, or even that it was a joke, in which case those listening might well decide that the speaker had gone a bit mad. Interruptions of course are a waste of time, as they cannot be interpreted.

Curious things can sometimes happen. With the German language the verb often does not appear until the end of the sentence, and I remember once at a Committee meeting a German member delivering a vigorous speech on some complicated financial subject. There was nothing to be heard on my headphones, and I was just about to point out to the Committee President that the system had broken down, when a plaintive voice in my ear said 'No verb yet.' Then a little later the voice said 'Still no verb!'

Finally the interpreter rattled through what the speaker had been saying before he finally produced the verb.

Only once did I see a complete breakdown in the process of interpretation. I was presiding at a Dinner of our Group in Aarhus, in Denmark, attended of course by our own Group members but also by a considerable number of what I took to be colleagues of our Mr Nyborg in the Danish 'No Tax' Party. To open the proceedings I made a speech of welcome, which I hoped would be the end of the speech-making for the night. But that was a foolish thought. One after the other thirteen speeches in Danish were made, each followed by a call of 'skol!' and a toast. They all had to be interpreted consecutively into French and English – in effect making 39 speeches in all. Each time the restaurant tried to bring in some food a new speech would start, so they finally implored us to halt the speechifying long enough for them to bring in the main course.

The final speech was made with great eloquence by a burly gentleman with what seemed like a rather thick accent. The only obvious word one could pick out at frequent intervals was 'Skol!' After he had finished the highly skilled interpreter stood up. 'I am very sorry,' she said, 'but I did not understand one single word of that.' In a way this little breakdown in the system was a reminder of how much we relied on our interpreters to enable us Parliamentarians to understand each other. Without them we would be lost.

Problems and Personalities

It was always interesting at the European Parliament to observe the very varied views held by members stemming from different parts of the Community. The four multi-national Political Groups were not Parties in our sense of the term; they were simply very loose coalitions. On really important issues, such as the election for President of Parliament, members were expected to back the Group decision – and there were ways of ensuring that they did so. On other issues, however, members could pretty well do as they liked.

Thus the 12 national parties represented in the Liberal Group ranged from a solitary Englishman whom one might describe as 'do-gooder left of centre', to a couple of Italians who were just about as far right as you could get. The big Christian Democrat Group included very conservative elements from Italy and from Bavaria in southern Germany; but other members were of a more moderate tendency, including those from our own Fine Gael Party. Some of the members of the Socialist Group could more accurately have been described as Social Democrats, others were much further to the left. As I have already mentioned, the French and Italian Communists were poles apart.

Such national differences one could understand. One could even understand – from long experience – that the British members were likely to have political views quite different from those held by anyone else. What is surprising is the double U-turn that has come about in those views. At the European Parliament in the 1970s the British Labour members were strongly opposed to the EEC, while the Conservatives were in favour. At the present day the Blair Labour Party is more or less pro-European, while the Tories have become increasingly 'Euro-sceptic'.

Such was the hostility of British Labour to the EEC that at the beginning of 1973 they refused to take their seats in the Parliament. The Tories therefore appointed just over half the British delegation and formed their own Group in the Parliament. All those appointed, naturally, were Conservative Party members, save for one Liberal and an Independent member called Lord O'Hagan. As an Independent he was given a seat in the back row in the 'hemicycle' (the hall where the Plenary Sessions were held). Presumably because he was a Lord he was placed at the extreme right, next to a couple of Italian neo-Fascists. As a result he wrote an angry letter to the Bureau complaining about this seating arrangement: he wanted, he said, to be placed as far left as was possible. They took him at his word, and he thenceforth sat next door to the Communists, where he was apparently very happy. Times change, however, and when ten years later I revisited the Parliament I noted that he had become a front bench member of the Conservative Group.

When the British Labour members did finally come to the Parliament they naturally joined the Socialist Group, but in a form of external association. They held their own private meetings and made their own decisions about how they would vote on all issues.

The Conservatives from the start made the right 'European' noises. Their leader, Peter Kirk, spoke immediately after me at the first Ceremonial Sitting and promised support for the work of the Parliament. It struck me as a little odd, however, that on his very first day in Strasbourg he listed the ways in which the procedures of the Parliament could be improved. He was sure, he said, that the European Parliament could learn from the experience of the House of Commons, and he had prepared a memorandum on this subject that he was sending to the Bureau. I never saw a copy of this memorandum, but it obviously had no effect, because Parliament's procedures remained quite unchanged.

Peter Kirk was a man one could admire, but not like. Highly intelligent, he had a cold and humourless personality, with a certain element of arrogance that one expects from Tories. But he had a superb grasp of procedure, for which I was prepared to forgive a lot. He realised fairly rapidly that no one at the Parliament was interested in the practices of the House of Commons. British entry to the EEC had come many years too late, and by the time they did arrive the procedures of the Parliament were firmly based on those of the Assemblée in Paris.

Once Kirk had accepted this fact, he settled in as a member of the Political Committee, to the production of a series of Reports setting out how the Parliament could bring about an increase in its powers simply by making better use of the powers it already possessed. Unfortunately these proposals had little effect, as the Continental parliamentarians preferred to make eloquent speeches demanding that the Council grant them extra powers. The fact – at that period – that there was no possibility of the Council agreeing to this did nothing to stem the flow of oratory.

In spite of all the 'European' speeches of the Conservative Group one always had a certain impression that the old imperial attitudes were not quite dead. Sometimes, quite unexpectedly, they would come out into the open. I was once at a meeting of the Bureau of the Parliament in Bonn, where we spent a weekend being entertained by the Christian Democrat Government. Those were the days of Margaret Thatcher's Government and the Conservatives were very anxious to ingratiate themselves with Helmut Kohl's Party members in Bonn. We had therefore several days of 'European' speechifying and general back-slapping between Peter Kirk and his German friends.

After the meeting we all headed for the Airport, and I travelled to London with Kirk and his Group colleague Lord Bessborough. They headed for the First Class section while I remained in 'steerage', but we met again at London Airport. How did they get on, I asked? 'Well,' Kirk said, 'at first we had the cabin to ourselves, but then along came two ghastly Krauts!' So much for the European ideal.

On another occasion the Bureau met in Berlin, and our meeting was held in the old Reichstag building. Amongst our number was a young Tory called Patrick Cormack, who had been just three weeks at the Parliament, but had been sent along by Peter Kirk to represent him. We had had a brief conversation before the meeting, in the course of which Cormack assured me that he could trace his family lineage back 1,000 years, and that in spite of his name there was not a drop of Irish blood in him.

At the start of the meeting we had the usual speech from the Mayor, welcoming us to the City and telling us all about the notorious Wall, that was just a couple of hundred metres away. In accordance with protocol the reply should have been given by the senior member present, but young Cormack leaped to his feet and said that, 'As the only member of the Mother of Parliaments present, I suppose I should reply to that.' And he did so, at some length.

Twenty years later Patrick Cormack is still in the House of Commons, and seems to have escaped even the recent disaster that befell the Conservative Party. So far as I know, however, in all that time he has never been promoted, a sign perhaps that the leaders of his Party have been able to recognise his true qualities.

Even after all the years during which we have been trying to deal with the British, they can still on occasion surprise us with their total inability to understand the realities of Anglo-Irish history. One such occasion was in 1976, at a conference in Abidjan in the Ivory Coast – an annual affair at which 60 members of the Parliament met representatives from the developing countries of Africa, the Caribbean and the Pacific area (known as the ACP countries). These representatives were all French-speaking, as the former British colonies had not yet entered the ACP system.

The opening day of this Conference was quite an Irish affair. I was heading Parliament's delegation so I made a speech, as did Dr Patrick Hillery on behalf of the Commission. Finally Garret FitzGerald spoke, as President of the Council. He speaks excellent French – with the same machine-gun rapidity as when he is speaking English – so he addressed the French-speaking delegates in their own language. As we normally do when addressing people from former colonial countries, he pointed out that we in Ireland, as a former colonial country ourselves, have a special understanding of their problems.

This harmless speech caused great excitement amongst the British Conservative delegates. After the inaugural meeting they were going around talking to each other with serious faces, much as if they had just heard that the Queen had died. I met one of them, a peer called Lord Reay. What was the problem, I asked. 'Well' he said, 'he spoke in French.' This was a serious charge; we English-speakers must stick together. But there was much worse: 'He said you were a former colony.' 'I thought we were' I said. 'Oh no, you were a part of the United Kingdom and you left us.' This would have been funny were it not so depressing. Even after 50 years these British Conservatives had not even the slightest understanding of the Irish case for independence. We had always felt we were a nation: to them we were merely a few British Counties that went astray.

The City of Abidjan was an interesting place, sky-scrapers everywhere, completely modern and European in appearance. The buses were identical with those in Paris, the supermarkets were filled with French goods, even to the counter laden with cream cakes. We could have been in any French city, save that all those in the streets and shops were African. There were hardly any Europeans: I had lunch one day with the entire Irish population of the Ivory Coast, a man and his wife.

While we were at the Conference we were brought to visit the 'President for Life', Houphuet-Boigny, in his beautiful palace. This had been designed by French architects, who had created a superb building, all in white, light, airy, with fountains playing everywhere. Our Gaullist colleagues told us that some time before, President de Gaulle had come on an official visit. He was of course shown round the palace, and he told the President for Life how much he admired it. 'But this must have been very expensive' he said, 'are you sure your people can afford it?' 'But, Mons. le Président, in France you have Versailles and Chambord and many other great palaces like them.' 'That is true,' replied de Gaulle, 'but we inherited these.' 'Ah yes, but one has to begin somewhere!'

This was a period when Fianna Fáil were out of office, having been replaced by the Coalition Government led by Liam Cosgrave. I was of course heavily involved back in Dublin in the Seanad, but so far as the European Parliament was concerned the change of Government would not normally have made much difference. Generally speaking, all the Irish members would hold the same views on matters of interest to Ireland, particularly agriculture and the Regional Fund. Yet at one stage in 1976, Richie Ryan as Minister for Finance issued a remarkable statement stating that 'Ireland's name on the international scene has been damaged by the irresponsible antics of the Fianna Fáil members of the European Parliament, who have abused their position in Europe to damage Ireland's reputation.'

The cause of all this excitement was a Resolution concerned with Equal Pay for women that I had tabled a few days earlier at the European Parliament, on behalf of our European Progressive Democrat Group. The Directive on Equal Pay had been signed in February 1975, by Garret FitzGerald in his capacity as President of the Council. This Directive had been drafted by Dr Patrick Hillery, as Commissioner in charge of Social Affairs, and was probably the most important decision ever taken by the EEC in this field.

As the months went by, however, the employers of Ireland convinced the Coalition Government that the immediate introduction of Equal Pay would result in general bankruptcy. Garret FitzGerald and Michael O'Leary (leader of the Labour Party) headed for Brussels to try to persuade the Commission to allow Ireland to postpone Equal Pay. O'Leary, incidentally, had come to the Parliament a few months earlier to speak with satisfaction of the progress that had been made with respect to women's rights.

Under the circumstances I felt that the European Parliament should use its influence against any delay in the introduction of Equal Pay. Not wishing to wash our national dirty linen in public, I drafted a non-controversial Resolution that made no mention of the Irish Government:

> *The European Parliament*
>
> 1. Welcomes the entry into force on February 10, 1976, of Equal Pay throughout the Community;
> 2. Welcomes the efforts so far made at national level to introduce the principle of Equal Pay into the legislation of the Member States;
> 3. Calls on all national Governments to ensure that there will be no delay in completing the introduction of Equal Pay for men and women throughout the nine Member States of the Community;
> 4. Urges the Commission to take all necessary steps to ensure the rapid and effective implementation of the Directive on Equal Pay in all Member States.

This was a mild Resolution indeed in comparison with a submission sent to the Brussels Commission on the very same day, by the Irish Congress of Trade Unions, which described the Government's behaviour on the Equal Pay issue as 'grossly retrogade', 'deplorable' and 'anti-democratic and a serious violation of civil liberty and human rights.' If I had included expressions such as these in my Resolution then Richie Ryan might really have had some cause for grievance.

In the event the Commission, by unanimous vote, refused to allow any delay in the introduction of Equal Pay. Ireland was not, after all, reduced to national bankruptcy. We Fianna Fáil members of the European Parliament resumed our efforts to encourage Community legislation that might be of benefit to Ireland, and we received no further rockets from Dublin.

From the start one of our aims had been to use the votes of our Group, whenever possible, to help with the economic and social development of Northern Ireland. Peter Kirk, when he first arrived at the Parliament, had said that his Tory delegation had been selected so as to represent every part of the United Kingdom. In fact this was less than accurate, as neither then nor at any time up to Direct Elections in 1979 was there any representative from Northern Ireland.

On one occasion this led to a serious confrontation between our two Groups. Brian Lenihan was speaking in support of an amendment we had put down to some Commission proposal, with a view to benefiting Northern Irish interests. In doing so he pointed out that, there being no members from Northern Ireland, it was up to us to protect their interests. This led to immediate Tory fury, and a public demand for an apology. So Brian returned to the Chamber, and said the same thing all over again.

For the last couple of years that I was at the Parliament I was a member of the Budget Committee. I was therefore able to take advantage of a rule under which a small sum could be added to the annual Budget of the Commission. Such an addition to the Budget was 'as of right' and, once decided by Parliament, could not be changed by the Council. I put down an amendment to include a sum in the Budget for 'Cross Border Studies', that would consider proposals that might lead to useful social and economic schemes being carried out in Border areas. There was general agreement with this proposal, but there was strong opposition from Tam Dalyell, a Scottish Labour member. He was that strange phenomenon, an old-Etonian Socialist, and a couple of years before he had succeeded (by a clever manipulation of the voting system) in preventing the establishment of a Scottish Assembly, in spite of there being a majority referendum vote in favour.

Dalyell opposed the whole concept of Cross-Border Studies on the grounds, he claimed, that anyone taking part in these would be in constant danger of being blown up. So great was the danger that it would be impossible to get anyone to take part in them. I replied, of course, that this suggestion was ridiculous. Upon this he called across the table to me to say 'You know, my constituents are being murdered in Aughnacloy.' My obvious reply would have been to suggest that it might be better if his constituents and their notoriously ill-behaved Scottish Regiment stayed at home. But this was not the time to be provocative, as I wanted to get my amendment through.

The Budget Committee duly accepted it, having decided that Tam Dalyell's fulminations should be ignored. In due course the amendment was accepted by Parliament in Plenary Session. The Cross-Border Studies got under way, and the first question studied concerned the possibility of re-opening the old canal linking the Shannon and the Erne. The new Shannon-Erne Waterway, opened in 1994, was the final result of my initiative.

The next matter concerning Northern Ireland with which I became involved was rather different. There was a constant stream of visiting groups from all countries of the EEC, subsidised by the Parliament to come to Strasbourg to see it in operation. Shortly before the 1979 Direct Elections one of these visiting groups was led by Ian Paisley, and I was asked to act as host on behalf of the Parliament.

The most important event during one of these visits was a meeting with representatives of each of the Parliament's Political Groups, who would explain their general outlook and the policies for which they stood. Paisley was very interested in this aspect of the visit, because he expected to be elected at the coming Direct Elections and wanted to know whether any of the Groups might suit his particular brand of politics.

He started in at once on the representative of the Christian Democrats who was not a Parliamentarian but a Dutch official of the Group. To Paisley, a Group that called itself Christian might have some virtues – but there was one matter that must be settled. What kind of Christian? 'How many Catholics are in your Group?' he asked the official, who had to admit he did not know. Paisley was incredulous: for an official not to know the number of Catholics in a Group for which he worked was clearly impossible. One sensed a feeling in the air that here was a Romish conspiracy to deceive these good Protestant men and women from 'Ulster'.

However, Paisley persevered. He had discovered that the Christian Democrat official was a Dutchman, so he started on a little Dutch history. You know, he said, that your William of Orange is our great Ulster hero? 'Amen' called a woman on his right who had a fanatical look. The official looked more confused than ever, There are at least a half-dozen Williams of Orange in Dutch history – all of them no doubt heroes to the Dutch. Which of them was this loud-voiced man talking about?

After this they got on to more practical matters, and the various members of the Paisley group asked me a series of questions about the economic and social policies of the EEC. Not surprisingly their interests were precisely those of the Irish delegation to the Parliament. One man made a long and indignant speech in which he launched a violent attack on the Government in London because, he claimed (probably rightly) they had used EEC funds intended for Northern Ireland in other parts of the United Kingdom. When he had finished I could only say that I did not think any of them would expect me to answer that.

This was the first time that I had met Paisley, and thinking about it afterwards I thought how alike are some of these loud-mouthed bigots. Paisley shares certain characteristics, for example, with the French right-winger Le Pen – venomous on a platform, but humorous and often quite likeable in private. I have heard it said, I don't know with what truth, that (as an MP) Paisley is helpful to all his constituents, of whatever religion. But get him on a platform – or a pulpit – and he is appalling.

We were now getting close to the end of the original nominated Parliament first established in 1958. It was now to be directly elected by the voters of each of the Member States. The final Plenary Session was held, and after that one final meeting of the Bureau. The President of Parliament, Emilio Colombo, was a native of Venice, so it was there that the Bureau meeting was held.

At the start of the meeting Colombo announced that the Sistine Choir from the Vatican was coming that evening to give a concert in St Mark's Cathedral. He suggested that we should all go, saying that the formal Dinner planned for the evening could be delayed until after the concert. So far as I was concerned, hearing the Sistine Choir in St Mark's was one of those events that happen only once in a lifetime. It was obvious that no one else shared this view, but it was accepted that if the President says we go to a concert, then we go. So that evening Gráinne and I joined the others in the front row in St Mark's.

During the interval a host of TV cameras appeared, and endlessly filmed Colombo in conversation with the local Cardinal. After this operation had been completed the sleek Parliamentary ushers in their white gloves appeared and said that now we would go to the Dinner. But, we protested, the second half of the concert had still to come; the Choir were to perform a Palestrina Mass. That was of no importance. The President was going, so we must also. We refused to budge, so everyone else trooped off to their water bus, and thence away to the Dinner.

It was obvious, of course, that Colombo's only purpose in going to the concert had been to be filmed with the Cardinal. Gráinne and I listened with intense enjoyment to the rest of the concert, and then took our own water bus to the ancient palace where the Dinner was being held. Formal Parliamentary dinners being what they are they had barely begun when we arrived, but as we marched up to the top table Colombo's looks were not exactly friendly.

A New Parliament

Once it had been decided by the Council that the first Direct Elections would be held in the year 1979, preparations for these got under way throughout the EEC. One obvious problem for us in Ireland was the matter of the new European constituencies. We had been allotted 15 seats in the new Parliament and, allowing for our multimember PR system, the constituencies were clearly going to be of enormous size.

There would obviously be less interest in a European election than there would be in a normal General Election. It would be hard to rouse any interest at all, unless voters could feel that they were electing people to the European Parliament from an area with which they could feel some sort of personal connection. This need became even clearer early in 1977, when the Cosgrave Coalition Minister for Local Government, Jim Tully, produced a Bill setting out his proposals for the new European constituencies – it was he who had invented the notorious 'Tullymander' of the Dáil constituencies.

The constituencies included in his new Bill made no sense at all. One of them, for example, extended from Wexford to Monaghan, ranging through various Midland Counties along the way. What possible feeling of common interest could there be amongst the voters in such a constituency? I was coming home one day from Strasbourg when I thought of the answer to the problem. Why not base the Euro-constituencies on Provincial boundaries? I made a rough calculation on the back of an envelope, and the figures seemed to work out all right.

When I got home I made some more detailed calculations and confirmed that the Euro-constituencies could indeed be arranged in this way. I gave the idea to the Fianna Fáil front bench and they agreed that this was the way we should go. A month or so later, however, Fianna Fáil returned to office and the new Government set up an independent commission to decide on the boundaries of the European constituencies. I made a submission to the commission, they accepted my suggestion, and that is the way the constituencies have been ever since: Munster, Connacht-Ulster, Dublin and the rest of Leinster. I can, I suppose, claim to be the only person who has ever produced a plan for constituency boundaries that was agreed without opposition from anybody!

The European Parliament itself was active in preparing for the Direct Elections. I myself was a good deal involved in this, largely because much of the work involved was within my particular area of expertise. The work of the Parliament was highly specialised, and Members became experts on such matters as the Budget, Agriculture, Social Affairs, the Regional Fund and the Environment. I had become an expert on Parliamentary Procedure, the drafting of new proposals and similar matters that became of special importance during this particular period.

One point that was naturally of major interest to all prospective candidates in the European election was that of the salary to be paid to the directly elected Members of the European Parliament (MEPs). In the nominated Parliament that existed from 1958 to 1979 there was no salary, but travelling and subsistence expenses were set much higher than actual costs, so that a member could emerge with a profit that did something to repay him for his labours.

This question of the MEPs' salary led to a great deal of discussion at the Bureau of Parliament. The basic problem was that Parliamentary salaries varied enormously in the nine Member States. The German and Italian salaries, for example, were about three times higher than that of a Dáil Deputy. The one thing on which everyone agreed was that in the new Parliament everyone should earn the same amount. It was not acceptable that two MEPs could sit side by side in Parliament of whom one would earn far more than the other. The Bureau discussions on this question continued for a number of meetings without any solution being reached.

In the end I produced a proposal to settle the issue. The salary for a member of the Belgian Chamber of Deputies was about the average for the Community, higher than in some countries, lower than in others. I suggested that we should decide on the Belgian salary level, but vary it up or down in accordance with differing costs of living in the various Member States. This is the system used for the salaries of Community officials.

This proposal was agreed by the Bureau, and sent off to the Council. It would probably have been accepted there, had it not been for the opposition of the British, who could not envisage a situation where their MEPs earned more than a member of the House of Commons! No common solution was therefore possible, so the Council decided that in each country parliamentary salaries would be the same at national and European levels. As a result, an Irish MEP, with the same salary as a Dáil Deputy, earns much less than his or her Continental colleagues. Now, twenty years later, the European Parliament has sent a new proposal for a common salary to the Council. This appears to be very similar to my suggestion that was adopted in 1978: it will be interesting to see what attitude the Council takes on this occasion.

One of the matters that had to be dealt with was the revision of the Rules of Procedure, to make provision for the new situation that would exist after Direct Elections. One obvious problem was that the new Parliament would have well over 500 members, twice the existing number, and many of the Rules would have to be amended to deal with this. I was therefore asked to draft a Report which would propose a complete revision of the existing Rules of Procedure.

I was very glad to be given this task, as it gave me the chance to make a number of changes that had nothing to do with Direct Elections, but which I had long felt to be badly needed. In particular I was determined to put an end to the interminable debates that took place each day on amendments to the Order of Business. Everyone had long agreed that these were intolerable, but when the Bureau, a year earlier, made a change in procedure it only made things worse. I therefore proposed an amendment to end all this time-wasting, and it was accepted by everyone.

Including that amendment we made some 45 changes in the Rules, all of which were accepted by Parliament in the Plenary session. One of the members of the Rules Committee, incidentally, was Jacques Santer, who is now President of the Commission. He used to present small technical amendments on behalf of the Christian Democrat Group, but I have no great memory of him, except as a pleasant but rather lightweight member of the Parliament.

Around the same period the Parliament decided to have three new officers called Quaestors (after the old Roman officials of that name) to look after all matters concerned with the well-being of the members. I was appointed one of these. Our remit covered a wide field, but the imminent Direct Elections were naturally our main concern.

The first item we had to deal with was the introduction of electronic voting. Until then voting in the Plenary Session had been by show of hands, but while it was just about possible to count 200 hands in the air, it would become impossible when there were over 500. In my innocence I assumed that there would be no difficulty in deciding on a suitable system of electronic voting. We would make inquiries, buy a system off the shelf, as it were, and that would be the end of it. I had not allowed for the ingenuity of politicians.

The principle of electronic voting is that at each member's seat there are three buttons representing 'Yes', 'No' and 'Abstain' (incidentally I have never understood what the distinction is between 'abstention', and simply not voting, but it is one beloved of all Continental parliamentarians). The basic problem with all such systems of voting is that it can be easy for a member to vote for an absent colleague. Our task as Quaestors was to find a fraud-proof system.

All sorts of ingenious ideas have been tried out. In the German Bundestag, for example, there was a complicated arrangement under which no vote was possible unless there was a weight of at least 30 kilograms on the seat concerned. So no one else could vote for an absent member. But we were warned against this system; there had been technical problems.

After a good deal of research we ended up in the Chamber of Deputies in Rome, where they had a straightforward system in which a light appeared (green, red, or white) as soon a member had voted. I cross-examined the Italian officials about the working of their system. Had there ever been any technical problems? None at all, they assured me: just on rare occasions when a member might get excited and pull out the wires. I thought it unlikely that there would ever be such excitement at the European Parliament.

We therefore recommended that the Italian system be used. It was duly installed in time for the inauguration of the new directly elected Parliament, and apparently worked very well. It proved itself early on when the President of one of the Political Groups was caught voting for an absent member. When taxed with this he explained somewhat implausibly that he had thought this was allowed.

Another matter with which the Quaestors had to deal was the construction of new buildings for the directly elected Parliament. There was a need for a whole range of Committee rooms and facilities for Members in Brussels, and a large building in Strasbourg for Members' offices. We were presented with the detailed plans, and these presented no problem. There was just one change we made in the Strasbourg plans. I insisted that provision must be made for a new restaurant, and this was agreed by the Mayor of Strasbourg, who was paying the capital cost of all this. This restaurant has been very popular – I claim that it should have been called the 'Yeats Restaurant'.

The new building proposed for Luxembourg was another matter. To begin with, it was not clear why the Luxembourg Government wanted to construct such a building, as it was several years since the Parliament had last met there, and it was extremely unlikely that it would wish to do so in the future. However that was not a question that concerned us. If the Grand Duchy of Luxembourg wanted a new building, then that was their decision: as Quaestors our duty was to ensure that it would suit the Parliament's needs – should there ever be such needs.

When we arrived in Luxembourg we were introduced to the architect from Paris, a Mons. Taillibert. We recognised the name at once: this was the man who had designed the famous (or notorious?) stadium for the 1976

Montreal Olympics, which had been brilliant in conception, accident-prone in use and inordinately expensive.

This time also, Taillibert had produced a remarkable design. The bottom of the building was more or less egg-shaped, and was to contain a hall to fit 600, as well as all the offices and facilities needed for Parliamentary sessions. From one side of the egg there jutted a slim 45-storey tower (for members' rooms), set at an angle of 45° to the ground.

Our immediate reaction when faced with a 500-foot tower sticking out at an angle was that it would fall down, but the architect assured us it would not. The egg-shaped part of the building, he claimed, would act as a balance. I wanted to know about the lifts in the 45-storey part of the building. How long would it take them to reach the top, since they would have to be pulled sideways rather than straight up and down, as is normal. They would be just as fast as a normal lift, I was told, though I was never quite convinced about this.

Speaking for myself, the more I saw of the plans, the more fascinated I became. This would clearly be a building such as had never been seen before. But now the problems began. The Grand Duchy of Luxembourg is a very small place and everyone knows what is going on. It seemed that everyone had seen the plans. The environment people led the way: with this enormous building sticking up from the Plateau of Kirchberg, the sacred soil of Luxembourg would never be the same again (that much was true anyway). My own view was that it would be the making of the Grand Duchy.

The City of Luxembourg is a place one can see in an afternoon; after that one might as well drive ten miles or so and have a look at Belgium, France or Germany. The 'leaning' Parliament building would have been an immense tourist attraction, as much a symbol of Luxembourg as the Eiffel Tower is of Paris. The environmentalists might in the end have been won over by such arguments, but there was more serious trouble to come.

The trade unions representing the staff of Parliament (all based locally) began agitating. Unfortunately the film 'Towering Inferno' had just arrived at the local cinemas: this was the film in which a very high building went on fire. This had convinced the staff that sky-scrapers were inevitably dangerous. 'Everybody knew' that any building over 15 stories was unsafe

– so much for Frankfurt or New York or Chicago. Anyhow, the leaning building would fall down. Even if none of these things happened, planes coming in to the local airport would certainly run into it.

But the Luxembourg Government stuck to its guns. They decided to go ahead with the leaning Parliament building, subject only to a survey by independent assessors. They employed a high-powered German company, and for a couple of months some 30 people looked into the whole thing. Then their report came back. The building was very well designed, it would not fall down, and it was perfectly suited to the needs of a Parliament. On the other hand, it would cost about six times more to build it than Mons. Taillibert had estimated. So that was the end of it. I have always regretted the loss of that 'Leaning Tower of Luxembourg'.

Finally we reached the day of the Direct Elections. In view of the extent to which I had been involved in the preparations for these elections, I suppose it is ironic that I should have failed in one basic task, that of getting myself elected. I had no difficulty in getting a Fianna Fáil nomination in the Dublin constituency, but in the campaign itself I fell far short of success. The European election as a whole was a catastrophe for Fianna Fáil. I had never felt particularly confident that I would be elected, but nonetheless it was a blow to have to leave a Parliament where I had spent by far the most interesting years of my political life.

Even though I was no longer a member of the Parliament, I was involved one last time in its affairs. As an outgoing Vice-President I was invited to attend the first meeting of the new Parliament. There was to be an opening Ceremonial Session with the usual formal speeches from everybody. Ireland at that moment held the Presidency of the EEC, and Jack Lynch was therefore due to speak for the Council.

One of the new members elected was Ian Paisley, and I felt certain that he would celebrate his arrival in Strasbourg by interrupting Jack Lynch during his speech. I therefore sought out Enrico Vinci, as by far the most intelligent of the senior officials of the Parliament (he is now Secretary General). I mentioned Paisley. 'What is a Paisley?' he asked. Vinci has a good command of English, but when someone is speaking in a language not his own there is always a possibility of confusion.

I explained that Paisley was a newly-elected member from Northern Ireland who had a political objection to the President of the Council (Jack Lynch) and would certainly embark on a speech of his own as soon as the President stood up. 'Ah', said Vinci, 'but that is not possible', and in his earnest bureaucratic way he went through the programme for the session. First there would be the speech from the President of Parliament, then the President of the Commission, then President Lynch, followed by speeches in turn from the President of each of the Political Groups. 'So you see,' he said, 'there is no possibility that this Mr Paisley can speak.'

I said that he could take it from me that Mr Paisley would certainly try to interrupt Mr Lynch. What needed to be done was to ensure that Paisley's microphone would not be activated. But, Vinci said, the President of the sitting has no button that he can press in order to deprive a member of his microphone (this indeed was a fault in the arrangements which has since been remedied). I said that somewhere there must be an official whose duty it was to activate a member's microphone when he embarked on a speech. He should be instructed that the Paisley microphone must remain dead. So we agreed to that, and I left.

The following day the Ceremonial Session got under way, and the time came for Jack Lynch to speak. As soon as he started there came the expected Paisley roar from the back bench. There was an immediate counter-roar from around 500 Parliamentarians, completely drowning out Paisley. The Irish present could of course recognise a Paisley when they saw one, but no one else had any idea what was happening, save that some lunatic was shouting from the back bench.

Without a microphone no one could use the headphones to hear what he was saying, nor was interpretation possible. Equally, there was no means of picking up his words for the Official Report. Paisley was filled with a righteous indignation, and I understand that when he reached home he went round telling his flock about the conspiracy against him that had been arranged in Rome – he has always been conscious of the fact that the European Parliament was set up under the Treaty of Rome. I don't suppose he has ever discovered that the 'conspiracy' was hatched by a Protestant from Dublin.

Brussels

After the European Elections I continued in politics for a while as a Senator, but then in April 1980 I moved to Brussels to take up a position as Director on the Secretariat of the Council of Ministers. I had of course been in Brussels many times before during my period at the European Parliament, but I had always stayed in hotels. Now for six years it became my home.

I rented a flat in Brussels, though of course we kept our house in Dublin and Gráinne commuted from time to time between one and the other. I had never lived in a flat before, and it took me a while to realise the implications of such a way of life. One evening I was happily typing a letter after midnight – I am often at my best at that hour – when the tenant from below came up in a rage and hammered on my door. It had never occurred to me that the noise from my typing would prevent him sleeping.

I think I was lucky in my neighbour, because the normal Brussels custom is not to protest directly, but to complain to the police. Everyone is allowed one annual party: you tell the police in advance, and then when your neighbours ring up to complain, the police look in their book and tell them your party is authorised. An Irishman living in Brussels told me he had his party one year, and as a gesture he invited all the other tenants in his apartment building. They listened to some loud disco music until everyone went home at 10.30 p.m.; then he himself went on playing the music. One of his former guests rang the police to complain; the party, after all, was over.

All this might suggest that the Brussels people are unfriendly, but I did not find them so. They are not in the least like the Parisians, who look with disdain on anyone who comes from elsewhere. In Brussels you will be greeted in a pleasant, friendly way, and they are happy when you speak French to them. In Paris they will sneer at your mistakes. On the other hand, in Belgium there is little sense of style, none of the French elegance. I feel that while one admires the French, it is often hard to like them: my view of the Belgians is the reverse.

Brussels is easy for a foreigner to live in, but it is definitely not a 'tourist' city. Once you have seen the Grande Place and the narrow streets round it, then that is it. The rest of Brussels is plain, often ugly. It is very easy to get around, because, to cater for visitors to a World's Fair some 40 years ago, they knocked down whole areas to create great boulevards that sweep through the city. But one should not complain: Paris is a wonderful city to visit, but I should hate to live there. I felt that if I had to live away from Dublin, then Brussels was as good a place as any.

Brussels is unique in Belgium in being officially bilingual. That is, almost everybody speaks French, but Flemish is given an equal status. All official signs must be in both languages. Thus in one large railway station there are 16 Flemish signs describing it as Schaarbeck and another 16 French ones calling it Schaerbeck, If the numbers did not balance exactly, there would be trouble. Everywhere else in Belgium a Commune is either Flemish or French, depending on which language is spoken by a majority. I once looked for a Customs form at the large Brussels International Airport at Zaventem and they gave me one in Flemish, so I asked for a copy in French. Impossible, they said, as Zaventem was a Flemish Commune. I would have to go back to the city to get a form in French.

I read one day in *Le Soir*, the Brussels daily paper, a curious story about a French-language school that for some historical reason was operating in a Flemish Commune (most of the outer suburbs of Brussels are Flemish speaking). The school had a problem, one that could only be solved by the municipal authorities. So they wrote to the Mayor – in French, of course, since they were a French-speaking school. The Mayor sent the letter back; as a Flemish-speaking Mayor he was not allowed to accept a letter in French. The school suggested a compromise: they would write letters in French, the Mayor could reply in Flemish. But no, that was impossible.

The school therefore decided to write to the Minister for Education – the French-speaking one of course – since there is one Education Minister for each language. I didn't know what good that would do. Could a French-speaking Minister write to a Flemish Mayor? The mind boggled. I never heard the end of the story, as it did not reappear in the columns of *Le Soir*.

My first encounter with the peculiarities of the Belgian language problem had been many years before while I was travelling by train to The Hague in the Netherlands. Whoever sold me the ticket had been under the impression that it was a through train. In fact I had to change three times, the last time being in Antwerp. I set out to find the train that would bring me to The Hague and, this being Belgium, I went round asking for information in French. No one would answer me, until I got to someone at an Information Desk, who was prepared to tell me (in English) where I could get my train. It was not until I came to live in Belgium that I realised that the one thing a foreigner must not do is speak French in a Flemish area. If you do you are met with immediate hostility: you have shown that you believe that all Belgians speak French.

Belgium is a sort of conservative oasis, surrounded by France, Germany and the Netherlands, countries that have a much more 'liberal' approach to modern living. This could cause problems, as I learned from another story in *Le Soir*. It seemed that each year at the summer season vast hordes of German tourists sped down the motorways to the North Sea beaches that run the full length of the Belgian coastline. There the women sunned themselves while topless, as was the custom where they came from, and from time to time they were hauled into Court by the Belgian police.

This was a distressing situation. First of all, one does not want to offend tourists who are a useful source of income. In addition, it upset the tidy Belgian mind that they were only prosecuted in certain areas, whereas in others they were left alone. So a high-level conference was held, bringing together the senior police officers from all the coastal Communes. After much discussion they came up with a new legal concept, what *Le Soir* described as 'Le toplessness, actif et passif'. In other words, so long as the topless remained motionless, the police would take no official notice.

Not all the stories about the Belgian police in *Le Soir* were at this frivolous level. They had a harrowing account one day of the arrest early one morning of a young Moroccan woman who was an illegal immigrant without papers. She spoke no French, but on her arrest she shouted at the police, gesticulated wildly and wept in anguish. The police paid no attention to all this, but lodged her in prison. Three weeks went by as the arrangements for her return to Morocco dragged on; she continued to be bitterly distressed. Finally someone arrived who was able to speak to her in her own language. The woman was trying to tell the police about her six-week-old baby that had been left behind in her flat.

Fortunately one of the woman's neighbours had noticed her disappearance and had taken in the baby. But as *Le Soir* pointed out, the information about the baby was in the woman's official police file, that no one had bothered to read. One would like to think that someone was censured for all this, but one doubts it. Poor immigrants do not get much sympathy in Brussels, where whole areas have been taken over by North Africans whose constantly noisy life-style does not fit in with a local ethos that says that you can only make noise once a year – and even then only with police permission.

Of course it is easy for an Irishman to be critical. We in Ireland have never until recently had to face the problem of large-scale immigration. Now because of our increasing wealth we are beginning to be of interest to immigrants from poor countries (such as Rumania). If this continues will we be any more sympathetic to them than are the Belgians? We must at least hope that if the day comes when the Gardaí have to start expelling illegal immigrants, they will do so with some degree of humanity.

If in Brussels there is a lack of sympathy with outsiders who are too poor, there is also an element of hostility to outsiders who are thought to be too rich – in other words, officials of the European Union. There is no doubt that EU salaries are high, but I think there is a reason for this. A Commission official said to me one day that he sometimes felt guilty about his salary, that he felt was too high for what he did. 'But of course,' he added 'I wouldn't be here if it wasn't.' These are people from all over Europe who have left their homes, their friends, to live in a strange country and, in many cases, to do all their work in a language not their own. Unless they were offered a higher salary, they would simply stay at home.

Under EU rules any official is entitled at all times to use his home language for his work, but the reality is somewhat different. At the Council the working language is French and all internal documents appear first in that language. The implications of this became clear during a labour dispute that erupted after I had been at the Council for a couple of years (as a Director I was 'invited' – i.e. directed – to stay at work). The Unions had decided that there would be a one-hour strike each morning and afternoon, the exact time of the stoppage being signalled by people trekking all over the building carrying cassette recorders playing Beethoven's 'Ode to Joy'. After a couple of months it became clear that this was futile; the work was getting done just as usual. So it was decided to inaugurate 'Opération Langue Maternelle': in other words, everyone was to do their work in their own language.

This would have been disastrous, as there no way that the translation service could have kept up with the work. All the multitudinous documents that are normally processed in French would have had to be translated into all the other EEC languages before work could even begin. But in fact 'Opération Langue Maternelle' was a total failure.

An Italian called Serafini who worked in my section came to me in a fury. He was a keen trade unionist, but he said the whole idea was ridiculous. He had been 20 years at the Council, had always worked in French. If he was made to do the work in Italian it would take him three times as long, as he knew none of the technical terminology except in French. He would have to spend all his time in the library looking up the Italian words. Like many other officials I myself had learned a peculiar sort of French. I could discuss EEC issues with fluency, but when I asked the concierge to clean my flat I had none of the right technical terms. To this day I don't know the French word for a sweeping brush.

Besides 'Community French', I absorbed a lot of other things during my first months at the Council. Having spent some years at the European Parliament I had a pretty good idea of the changes in the European power structure that had taken place in the years since the EEC was founded. But it was only when I came to work in the Council building in Brussels that I was able to observe at first hand how some of these changes had affected the lives of ordinary citizens of the Community. I came to know, for example, that on a day when there was to be a meeting of the Agricultural Council, we all entered the building through the back door: the open space at the front of the building was likely to be packed with demonstrating farmers from all over the Community.

Looking out one day at the sea of demonstrators bearing placards, I could see a group from Connacht, alongside others from Sicily, Normandy, Bavaria and many other places, In the old days Irish farmers came to Dublin to demonstrate or, in one famous case, to sleep for weeks on the Minister for Agriculture's doorstep in Government Buildings. Now they came to Brussels, where the power lay.

The most famous farmers' demonstration of all took place in the early EEC years, long before we had joined. Some Italian farmers brought a cow with them to Brussels, by some means got the animal past security and into the lift, and brought it up to the 13th floor where the Council of Agricultural Ministers was meeting. There is a wonderful photograph of the scene still to be seen here and there, pinned on a wall, showing the German Minister for Agriculture (who was presiding over the Council) trying to look cool and unconcerned while a large, sleek cow nibbled at his right ear.

Agriculture is perhaps a special case, in that the Common Agricultural Policy (CAP) is one of the most fully developed of all the policies of the EU. Other economic sectors are still largely dealt with at national level. This was and still is so with regard to Energy and Research, with which I was at first concerned when I joined the Council Secretariat. After a couple of years, however, I was put in charge of another Directorate, a move that brought me back to the scene I had known so well in former years. I was now dealing with relations between the Council and the European Parliament. I had spent some years as a member of the Parliament looking with deep suspicion on the Council. Now that I had, as it were, joined the enemy, I learned without any real surprise about the true attitude of the Council to the Parliament.

The essential democratic basis of the Community was that before enacting legislation the Council must first consult the Parliament – and the 'consultation' process was not finished until the Opinion of Parliament had been received. I myself could remember long hours at Committee meetings of the Parliament during which these Opinions were being drafted. There would be animated discussions as to the precise terms we should use. Should the proposed legislation be 'deplored', or 'regretted', or even 'condemned'? From time to time I had wondered whether all this was a waste of time, since the Council in any event would presumably not accept our views.

It was only when I joined the Council Secretariat that I realised how wrong I had been. I had assumed that the Council would read our so carefully drafted Opinions, and then reject them. I was now to discover the sad reality, that Parliament's Opinions were not read at all. After each Plenary Session I would be telephoned by officials from other Directorates of the Council. Had Parliament given its Opinion on such and such a matter? Yes, it had. 'Oh good,' they would say, 'then we can take a decision at the Council tomorrow.' There was no need to read the Opinion: its mere existence was enough. This was typical of the attitude of the Council at that period. The general principle seems to have been to give the European Parliament very little power, and then to restrict so far as possible the use of that power.

To my mind one of the least satisfactory aspects of Council-Parliament relations was the Question Time process, under which Members of Parliament could put down questions (for oral answer) demanding information about Council's actions and policies. It was only when I myself became responsible for the preparation of the answers to these questions that I realised just how unsatisfactory the system was (and I doubt if there has been any change since I retired from the Council Secretariat in 1986).

Once a Question has been put down by a Member, Council officials will draft a reply, conveying the minimum possible amount of actual information. This draft must then be accepted by the delegates of each Member State, who go to work with enthusiasm, cutting out a bit here and a bit there, so that in the end the answer even to a complicated Question may consist of just three lines. This answer has to be given in Parliament by a Minister representing whatever Member State has the Presidency of the Council. Ministers often complain about the brevity of these answers and, in certain cases, they deal with the situation by producing their own version off the cuff. This completely new answer that hasn't been seen by anybody, is then presented to the European Parliament as the considered unanimous view of the Member States.

On behalf of the Council I attended all sittings of the European Parliament. I would hear Members making speeches attacking the Council which seemed identical to those I used to make in my own days at the Parliament. I also went to all meetings of the Bureau in order to be able to give the viewpoint of Council on such matters as the dates and times of the appearances of Ministers.

In one respect at least, little seemed to have changed over the years. At the very first meeting of the Bureau I attended, in January, 1973, there was a letter from the Liberal Group complaining about their position on the extreme right of the Parliamentary Chamber, and asking to be moved towards the centre. Their request was refused – largely because no one else was prepared to be shifted to the right in their place. The last meeting of the Bureau I ever attended, this time representing the Council, was in January 1986, just before I retired. On this occasion also there was a letter from the Liberal Group asking to be moved away from the extreme right of the Chamber. But this time the Bureau agreed to their request.

On one occasion while I was at the Council I attended a meeting of the Parliament's Political Affairs Committee. Ireland had the Presidency of the EEC, so the Committee was to be addressed by Peter Barry – as President of the Council – in Dublin Castle. When I got there I found my old acquaintance Ian Paisley in fine form, stamping up and down and announcing to the world in general that he was going to interrupt Peter Barry and get himself thrown out of the meeting. 'Oh no,' I said, 'We'd never throw you out, not when you're at home!' 'I'm not at home, I'm not at home' said Paisley. In due course Peter Barry appeared and made his speech, but for whatever reason Ian Paisley stayed silent all through the meeting.

There is just one thing more that I feel should be said about the European Parliament. When I spoke for the Irish delegation at the Ceremonial Sitting in January 1973, I expressed the hope that the Parliament would 'become a fully equal partner with the other Community institutions.' This has not happened, but the Parliament has in fact greatly strengthened its position in the past few years. It received a number of extra powers under the Maastricht Treaty and again at the Amsterdam Summit in 1997. There has been a considerable change in the balance of power between Parliament and Council.

On the other hand there has been some weakening in the position of the 15 Irish MEPs. There are now over 600 members of the Parliament, and this number will rise still further if all six of the countries now negotiating for membership succeed in their aim. In that event the total number of MEPs would rise to around 770: but since it has been agreed that the figure of 700 seats in Parliament may not be exceeded, there would have to be cuts totalling around 70 in the size of existing delegations. We could find ourselves, therefore, with 14 instead of 15 MEPs – with further cuts to come in later years as yet further new countries line up to join the EU. In such a Parliament, with perhaps as few as 12 seats out of 700, we will have a very weak voice indeed.

There is certainly a need for greater democracy in the European Union, and the Parliament will always be an essential reflection of that democracy. But in the years to come we in Ireland must make sure that we do not give up the right to defend our own national interests. We must insist that such a European democracy must continue to have two aspects: the Parliament, representing the peoples of Europe as a whole, and the Council, representing the Member States and in particular the interests of the smallest amongst them.

Years of Change

When I look around me nowadays I am astonished at the changes that have come about in my lifetime. One must not be complacent: there is still an uneven distribution of wealth, there are pockets of severe unemployment, many things still remain to be done. But when I remember the conditions that existed when I first became active in public life in the 1950s, I rejoice that I have lived to see the Ireland of today.

As I write these words, some 65,000 young people await the Leaving Certificate results that in many cases will decide the course of their future careers. The most recent figures show that 81 per cent of all Irish children now remain on in school until the age of 17 to 19 – one of the highest proportions in Europe. Most of these students will continue their education at third level. I cast my mind back to the year 1955 when, as Secretary of a Fianna Fáil research committee, I first became actively interested in the educational system. One of the basic facts we had to deal with was that each year some 80 per cent to 90 per cent of children finished their education at the age of 14.

Those few who stayed on after that age were mostly the children of middle-class parents, who could afford to pay secondary school fees. Perhaps 5 per cent went on to University. But the great majority of Irish children emerged from school with only a minimum of education, and were thrown onto the labour market totally unskilled. At that time it was estimated that of those leaving school each year at the age of 14, about two-thirds would have emigrated within five years. They went to England, to take up the most menial and ill-paid jobs available.

Emigration nowadays is a different matter. The young people who go to Britain or to other countries in Europe, or to the USA, are well educated, more often than not with University degrees. For many years it was an accepted fact of economic life that emigration was inevitable. There simply was not enough work at home for all our people. All this has changed, and emigration has become a two-way movement. People leave to gain experience or to see what life is like outside our island, then come home again. In each of the last five years about 5,000 more have returned to Ireland than have left.

Other things also, have changed in the Ireland of today. Forty years ago more than half the population lived in rural areas, most of them on small farms bringing in (in pre-EEC days) a low and uncertain income. Living conditions were poor, farm houses had neither running water nor electricity. For the children growing up there was sometimes the chance of getting a job in a local factory, where such existed. There were just a few recognised sources of permanent employment – the Civil Service, the Banks, the Gardaí, teaching – but these all required a standard of education beyond that attained by most people. The emigrant ship remained the essential focus of economic life.

Much of this, of course, applied also in urban areas. There was high unemployment and a great deal of poverty – but even so conditions were better than for those on the land. I remember a Dáil Deputy from a Dublin constituency telling me once that farmers were no longer poor. He had been on holiday in the country, and had noticed that on Sundays some of the farmers were now coming to Mass in motor cars. He was almost indignant at the thought of such affluence. I suggested that Dubliners had been driving to Mass for years, so why not the farming community; but he was not mollified. He had always thought of farmers as being poverty-stricken, and could not adjust his mind to accept that things might at last be changing.

Things have, of course, been changing, at first slowly and hesitantly, more recently with extraordinary rapidity. Almost overnight, as it were, we have gone from being the 'poor man' of the EEC on our entry 25 years ago, to our present status as the 'Celtic Tiger', with a rate of economic growth far higher than that of any other European country.

There is just one aspect of the national scene that has changed very little – the political system. I myself first took an interest in politics around the time that Fianna Fáil and Eamon de Valera first came to power. In the 65 years since then the basic configuration of our Party system has remained quite unchanged. Throughout all this period Fianna Fáil has been the biggest Party, followed by Fine Gael, with Labour as a weak third Party: there have been numerous minor Parties, none of which has existed for long. I doubt if there is any other country that has had such a consistent electoral pattern over such a long period.

However, looking back at a lifetime spent as a 'Party hack', I can say that even if election results have varied little, campaigning methods have changed a great deal, as have the attitudes of voters. In the old days we took politics much more seriously than now. I remember the great election meetings in Dublin addressed by de Valera, with 50,000 or more in attendance, all of them enthusiastic Fianna Fáilers. In those days once you joined one of these mass meetings you stayed there: any attempt to leave while 'Dev' was speaking was met by a quiet closing in of the crowd. Nothing was said, but no one would be allowed to leave the meeting until the speech had been finished. It was accepted that Fianna Fáil was not a Party, but a Movement: a true Fianna Fáil supporter in those days would never vote for anyone else. If at an election he felt really aggrieved, then he might stay at home and not vote for anyone, that was as far as he would go.

The Labour Deputy Jim Tully told me a story once of an old man, a Fianna Fáil constituent of his in County Meath. According to Tully the old man was ill, and needed to go into hospital. But he couldn't get a bed there, so he tried the local Councillor and then the Fianna Fáil TD. They had no success, and finally he got very ill indeed, so in a panic he sought out Jim Tully. Either by luck or through greater efficiency, Tully managed to get him into hospital and in due course he was cured. The old man was very grateful, and a few weeks later one of Tully's supporters heard him in his local pub telling everyone about it. He sang the praises of Deputy Tully, who had saved his life, finishing by saying 'Isn't it a terrible pity he's not a Fianna Fáil man so that I could vote for him!'

True or not, that story did reflect the attitude of a typical Fianna Fáil voter in the old days, particularly in rural areas. In Dublin, voting patterns were often more fluid: as de Valera said himself, 'the Dublin people were always very flighty.' Nowadays the country as a whole is 'flighty', and voters tend to decide anew at each election how they are going to vote. In my younger days such an attitude would have been considered unworthy of a true Fianna Fáil supporter.

One aspect of the greater sophistication of the electorate today is that women play a greater part in political life. I remember one day in the 1940s when I was still a student in Trinity College; a friend and I had been to a public meeting in the Mansion House in Dublin. As we left the meeting he asked me, why did I think there were so few women in public life? Always happy to air my opinions, I said the answer was simple: there was no particular reason why the men should vote for them, and the women themselves wouldn't be seen dead voting for their own sex.

Thereupon a voice from over my right shoulder said 'I'm very interested to hear you say that. I'm a candidate in the local elections.' This was Helen Chenevix, one of the most prominent women trade unionists of the day. I retreated in some dismay, but I kept an eye on the Chenevix vote at the local election three weeks later. She got just 500 votes.

Indeed over a period of 50 years (with just one exception) no women were elected to the Dáil other than Deputies' widows, usually in by-elections, when they could count on a sympathy vote. The exception was Mrs Maureen O'Carroll, who won a seat for Labour in Dublin in 1954. It would be fair to describe this as a fluke: she got 1443 first preference votes (7 per cent of the total), and was never re-elected.

Women of course were active in all political parties. They made tea, addressed envelopes, sometimes rose even further in the ranks, but were not looked on as election material. It was assumed that they voted the same way as their husbands, and they were not expected to hold any political views of their own. As recently as the 1970s, Gráinne and I, at a European Parliament reception, were amongst a group of the Irish members who were discussing some political issue. Gráinne made some comment, upon which one of the group said in surprise 'Gráinne, I didn't know you were interested in politics.'

There is no doubt that women were in some respects looked on as inferior. The concept began early. In the last year of the National Schools curriculum, the boys did a little elementary algebra and geometry; the girls were excluded from these 'difficult' subjects, but did Home Economics instead. When one of our own children was preparing for the Leaving Certificate in a Dublin girls' school, the whole class – as was the custom – took the lower Mathematics course. Only when we complained did the school do a census, to find to their amazement that eight of the girls were able and willing to take the Honours course. A special class was set up for them, and most of them did extremely well.

After leaving school, the 'inferiority' of women continued to be a factor in their careers. For well over a century, all the bank cashiers in Ireland were male; not one single woman was allowed to hold this well-paid job. The women's organisations began complaining about this inequality, but were countered by a statement issued by the Governors of the various banks. It was impossible to employ women as cashiers, as the depositors would no longer have confidence in the safety of their money. Not until the 1970s was this position ended.

An equally idiotic statement was made on television by the late Charles Mitchel, the first (and perhaps the best-loved) RTÉ News announcer. He said he had been asked by various people why there were no women reading the news. The answer was simple: 'People would not believe the news if read by women.'

To be fair, it was not only in Ireland that doubts were held about the ability of women. I was at a meeting once of a European Parliament committee which was discussing a proposal sent to us by Paddy Hillery (Commissioner in charge of Social Affairs) dealing with equal opportunities for women workers. Objections were raised by a prominent Italian Communist who said that equality for women was impossible. No woman could drive a lorry, for example. I said I couldn't see any problem, in these days of power steering. Anyhow, I added, we now even have commercial passenger planes with women pilots. He was amazed to hear this, and I thought somewhat alarmed. I felt he would be very unwilling to travel in any plane piloted by a woman.

On another occasion at the European Parliament, there was a senior position to be filled, and a board was set up to interview a number of candidates. In due course an appointment (male) was made, and some time later I was told about the various interviews by a member of the board. One particular female candidate, he said, was by far the best, 'but of course we couldn't appoint her.' To be fair, this was not typical of the Parliament's recruitment practices. But it is in fact only recently that women have been gaining access to the top positions in the civil service of the EU.

As we approach the Millenium, however, the general position of women has certainly improved compared with former years. In the political field there has been a big increase in the number of women who gain election to the Dáil – and the Presidential election of October, 1997, showed that there is no longer any bias amongst the voters against women candidates. The four women who sought the Presidency got over 95 per cent of the total vote, the rest being garnered by the solitary male, Dermot Nally. It has taken a long time, but any woman who wants to stand for election is now able to do so on a basis of equality with the men.

There is just one further matter I should like to deal with before closing this final chapter, on the 'Years of Change'. It is now exactly 25 years since we became members of the EEC on 1 January 1973. To what extent has the Community been responsible for our present status as the 'Celtic Tiger'? In the first place it is clear that our recent economic development would have been impossible without the existence of a well-educated labour force, providing the range of skills needed by the new industries being set up in Ireland. On the other hand it is also clear that these industries would not have come here in the first place, were it not for our membership of the European Union, giving us free access to Continental markets. We are told that one half of all computer software sold in Europe is made in Ireland – a telling example of the new position we hold in the modern world.

We will of course continue to benefit from our membership of the immense European free trade area, but we must expect a phasing out of the Structural and other payments we have been receiving from Brussels. When we joined in 1973 we had by far the weakest economy of any Member State of the EEC. Many people in Europe, I think, looked on us in the earlier years of our membership as a sort of poor relation of the United

Kingdom, adept at flourishing the begging bowl and with little positive to contribute. All this has changed, and our living standards are now close to the average of the European Union. The penalty of our success will be that we will be expected to pay our own way in Europe.

To my mind this is not a matter of regret, but of jubilation. In the 70 years since Independence we had come to accept that we lagged behind other countries, that our economy was weaker, our living standards were lower. We blamed all this on our former colonial status, on our lack of natural resources, on our continued domination by Britain's industrial might. All this is in the past. In joining the Community in 1973 we gave up an element in our political independence, but now, 25 years later, our position in the world has changed completely. With our new-found economic strength and prosperity, we have become, for the first time, a truly independent nation.

Index of Names